# chase

chasing after the heart of **God**

**AN EIGHT-SESSION BIBLE STUDY**

## jennie allen

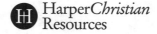
Harper*Christian* Resources

*Chase Study Guide*
© 2012 by Jennie Allen

Published in Grand Rapids, Michigan, by HarperChristian Resources.
HarperChristian Resources is a registered trademark of HarperCollins Christian
Publishing, Inc.

Requests for information should be sent to customercare@harpercollins.com.

ISBN 978-0-310-17027-3 (softcover)
ISBN 978-0-310-17028-0 (ebook)

HarperChristian Resources titles may be purchased in bulk for church, business,
fundraising, or ministry use. For information, please e-mail ResourceSpecialist@
ChurchSource.com.

Author image © Jessica Taylor. Used with permission.

First Printing October 2012 / Printed in the United States of America

*She will chase after her lovers but not catch them; she will look for them but not find them.*

**hosea** 2:7 NIV

# contents

# acknowledgments

I want to thank some of the people who have invested in my life and pushed me to chase God.

Fellowship Bible Church in Little Rock—thank you for raising me in my faith.

Ann Parkinson modeled passionately loved people and Jesus for me as I was growing up.

Joe White's passion for God is contagious and it lit something in me as a teenager at Kanakuk Kamps.

Michelle Bost, you showed me what discipleship looked like during my years in college through CRU. Thank you, Michelle and CRU.

Beth Moore, your passion for God showed me I wasn't crazy. And as a female teacher of God's Word, I stand on your shoulders.

Thank you for obeying God with your life and ministry.

Glenn Kreider expanded my view of God and made me fall in love with studying God in my years at Dallas Theological Seminary. Thank you Dr. K and DTS.

Karen Freisen and Gayle Clark, you keep me chasing God. You are friends and mentors at the same time.

Austin Stone Community Church—you raise the bar of what it means to follow Jesus. I run faster today because of you. Honored to be led by the most passionate and God-fearing people I know.

And of course thank you to my parents, Carolyn and Bill Stowers, and to my husband, Zac, you continue to show me God everyday! Thank you for your investment in my life.

Finally, to the many women who sat on living room floors the very first Chase and watched a mess of a girl try to figure out God, you are a part of these words. Thank you for wrestling through this with me. Thank you for chasing God alongside me.

There are too many to name. But I pray you know your faith has fallen into my life and made me see God. Thank you.

# introduction

I was eighteen years old. I felt paralyzed in my relationship with God. I knew God was real, but my fancy prayers and daily devotionals were not cutting it. I was doing everything right, but it felt all wrong. Yet I thought I was giving God what He wanted.

I began to question—and this good little Bible-belt girl somehow missed the rules for wrestling with her God. As I surveyed my life, I realized doing all the right things had won me the admiration of everyone but God. And I felt empty and prideful. It was worse than rebellion: being good with no God. It was beginning to occur to me maybe God was after something else.

Maybe I was chasing the wrong things.

And then I stumbled across a phrase in 1 Samuel 13.

David was "a man after [God's] own heart" (v. 14).

The phrase intrigued me because I knew David committed murder and adultery—he was no missionary or priest. I saw this man as both completely sold out for God and completely broken. He was in love with God. He lived with an acute awareness of his need for Him.

The closer I have gotten to the life of this man, David, the more my ideas of what God wants from me have been shattered. David had one life and two eyes and one heart, just like me, but they were all laser-focused on the heart of his God . . . my God. David was in love with Him.

And, yes, David sinned and wrestled, just like me. But while he was not so concerned about appearing godly, he was terribly concerned about knowing God. He was a man who saw past his circumstances, past himself, past this life to the heart of God.

## We gather together to discover the heart of God.

I am terrified we get it wrong a lot of the time. We rarely, in our busy lives, stop and see Him, *really* see Him. We are so busy doing things for Him and for everyone else we altogether miss Him. He wants *us*.

As we chase after His heart together for these few short weeks, we will explore the life of David, a man who knew the heart of God. We will look into their passionate conversations. And whether you are running from God or working your tail off to please Him, David's journey will challenge your view of God.

The story of David's life and his prayers fill God's Word. It's as if God was saying, *When you open My Word, look at this man, look at his prayers, look at his life, look at his mistakes, look at his faith, and you'll see Me, My heart*.

Let's chase.

*Jennie*

# instructions and expectations

## What do you hope to get out of this study?

_____

_____

_____

_____

## Engage with Your Small Group

An important part of personal growth is community. We are going to deal with the way we view God and how our hearts can change to be more like His. This could be a painful process and it will certainly reveal sin in all of us. Make sure you have a group of women to walk through this process with you.

## Commit to Being Consistent and Present

The nature of life makes it nearly impossible to follow through with a thorough examination of our hearts and Scripture—not to mention the devil's desire to interfere with it. Commit to being present at your group meetings, barring an emergency, and arrange your schedule so you do not miss any part in this journey. Have your lesson and projects finished when you come to the group meeting.

# Ground Rules
# for Group Discussion Time

:: *Be concise.* Share your answers to the questions while protecting others' time for sharing. Be thoughtful. Don't be afraid to share with the group, but try not to dominate the conversation.

:: *Keep group members' stories confidential.* Many things your group members share are things they are choosing to share with you, not with your husband or other friends. Protect each other by not allowing anything shared in the group to leave the group.

:: *Rely on Scripture for truth.* We are prone to use conventional, worldly wisdom as truth. While there is value in that, this is not the place. If you feel led to respond, please only respond with God's truth and Word, not "advice."

:: *No counseling.* Protect the group by not directing all attention on solving one person's problem. This is the place for confessing and discovery and applying truth together as a group. Your group leader will be able to direct you to more help outside the group time if you need it. Don't be afraid to ask for help.

# Study Design

In the first meeting, your groups' study guides will be passed out and you will work through the Getting Started lesson together. After that, each lesson in the study guide is meant to be completed on your own during the week before coming to the group meeting.

These lessons may feel different from studies you have done in the past. They are very interactive. The beginning of each lesson will involve you, your Bible, and a pen, working through Scripture and listening to God's voice. Each lesson will conclude with four projects you can do to help you further process how to live God's Word. Don't feel as if each lesson has to be finished in one sitting; take a few blocks of time throughout the week if you need to.

The goal of this study is to dig deeply into Scripture and uncover how it applies to your life, *to deeply engage the mind and the heart.* Projects, stories, and Bible study all play a role in it. You may be drawing or journaling or interacting with the homeless. At each group meeting you will discuss your experience in working through that week's lesson.

# Terrific Resources for Further Personal Study

biblegateway.com
bestcommentaries.com

# Who Is David and Why Does He Matter?

A. Who was David in history?

1. David was the second king of Israel.

2. He is said to have lived around 1040–970 BC.

3. His reign lasted a total of forty years.

4. David made Jerusalem the capital of Israel after he defeated the Jebusites who inhabited it.

5. David's reign can be divided into two segments. For the first seven years he reigned over Judah because the nation of Israel had been divided into two parts: Israel in the north and Judah in the south. Eventually, the kingdom was reunited and David reigned over it for thirty-three years.

B. Who is David in Scripture?

1. David is a king in the Old Testament. His life is primarily documented in 1 and 2 Samuel, concluding in 1 Kings.

2. At first, David was a shepherd, the youngest son of Jesse. However, God withdrew His favor from the current king, King Saul, and chose David to be the new king. God accomplished this by sending His prophet, Samuel, to choose a new king from among Jesse's sons.

3. David became Saul's armor-bearer. He then made a name for himself by defending Israel against the Philistines and defeating Goliath.

4. David became commander over Saul's armies and married Saul's daughter, Michal. He rose in popularity and Saul became jealous.

5. Saul plotted David's death, but David was warned by Saul's son, Jonathan, and fled into the desert. It was during this time in the wilderness that David penned many of the Psalms.

6. Both Saul and Jonathan were killed in battle against the Philistines, and David returned to be crowned as king of Judah.

7. The second half of David's life was marked by tragedy after he committed adultery with Bathsheba, had her husband killed, and was rebuked by the prophet Nathan. As a consequence of his actions, the first child born to David and Bathsheba died.

8. Bathsheba's second son to David would be Solomon. Solomon became the next king and was reputed for his wisdom, wealth, and power. Solomon also wrote Proverbs, Ecclesiastes, and Song of Solomon.

C.  Who is David in God's plan?

1.  David revealed God's character and plans for Israel.

    a. The story of David is part of a larger story that begins in Genesis and recounts the history of Israel. As Israel developed into a nation and established its identity, it continually chose an identity apart from God. Israel chose an earthly king as its ruler (a symbolic rejection of God and His sovereignty), so God used David to display His character and plans.

    b. "Thus Saul, designated by God at the people's insistence, must be rejected in favor of David, the one whom God chose freely."[1]

2.  David's life ultimately pointed to Jesus Christ.

    a. During David's reign, God made a covenant with him, promising that He would establish the house of David eternally: "Your throne shall be established forever" (2 Samuel 7:16).

    b. This covenant was fulfilled through Christ, who is referred to as the "Son of David" (Luke 18:39), "the root of David" (Revelation 5:5), and "the Offspring of David" (Revelation 22:16 NIV).

    c. David is an ancestor of Jesus Christ through both Mary and Joseph.

*Summary*: Scripture paints for us a picture of a complex man who was heroic and merciful yet "adept at clothing his power-seeking and self-interest in the rhetoric of piety and morality."[2] It is clear from David's actions, however, that he was not chosen because of his inherent goodness. David was chosen because of God's goodness. God is able to use anyone redemptively that He so chooses.

## David's Psalms: Where Did They Come From? What Are They?

### General Info

::  The word *psalms* is derived from the Greek word *psalmos*, which is translated from the Hebrew *mizmor. Mizmor* "signifies music accompanied by stringed instruments."[3]

::  The word *psalm* later came to mean a "song of praise." In the Hebrew Bible, the title of the book of Psalms is *seper t'hillim*, which means "Book of Praises," referring to their content rather than their form.[4]

::  The Psalms are the largest collection of ancient lyric poetry in existence. Lyric poetry "directly expresses the individual emotions of the poet."[5]

::  "They reveal all the religious feelings of the faithful—fears, doubts, and tragedies, as well as triumphs, joys, and hopes."[6]

:: The Psalms formed the "hymnal" of the temple, which is why they often celebrate ordinances of the sanctuary.

:: Types of psalms: lament, thanksgiving, and descriptive praise.

## David's Psalms

:: Seventy-three of the psalms are credited to David.

:: David was a musician. Scripture tells us David was a singer of songs and the primary organizer of musical guilds for the sanctuary (1 Chronicles 15:3–28; 16:4–43; 23:1–5; 2 Samuel 6:5). He famously soothed King Saul with his music (1 Samuel 16:17–23).

:: The Psalms were forged amidst David's varying life circumstances. Consistent with the lyric poetry genre, the psalms express the deep emotions of David. They are often raw and angry, but they are also honest and faithful.

:: Walter Brueggemann says: "The Psalms transmit to us ways of speaking that are appropriate to the extremities of human experience."[7]

1 Bruce M. Metzger and Michael D. Coogan, eds., *The Oxford Guide to People & Places of the Bible* (Oxford: Oxford University Press, 2001), 53.
2 Ibid., 52.
3 Allen P. Ross, "Psalms," *The Bible Knowledge Commentary: Old Testament*, ed. John F. Walvoord and Roy B. Zuck, (Colorado Springs: Cook Communications Ministries, 2004), 779.
4 Ibid.
5 Ibid.
6 Ibid.
7 Walter Brueggemann, *The Psalms and the Life of Faith* (Minneapolis:Fortress Press, 1995), 27.

# getting started : chase :: 1

*After chasing everything the world has to offer, nothing is more satisfying than God.*

Pages 20–25 are intended for you to get acclimated to this study on your own, after you watch the first video. Flip to page 26 for Video Teaching.

# What Do We Chase?

Tell me how to please God.

There are days my mind and heart race anxiously at the thought I may be terribly off track in that sincere pursuit. Most days I want to please God. I believe He is real and I believe a day is coming when I will face Him. I want, more than any other thing, for that day to go rather spectacularly. I don't want to be shocked when I am looking into the face of the God of the universe to find I actually missed the point.

One of the great fears of my life is that I would get to the end of my life and realize I lived for the wrong things.

But there are also the days I forget that all the invisible stuff is real, and pleasing God is far from my thoughts and I just chase whatever I want, whatever seems to feel right in the moment. I seek happiness through friends or food or my kids or the approval of people or wasting minutes on Facebook or catching up on shows on Hulu. There are unending distractions to chase.

And then there are the days when I am not chasing meaningless distractions, I am flat-out running from God, arms full of sin.

This study is a story about our God using a man who not only questioned Him but also sinned so atrociously most present-day Christians would avoid him. Yet David at the same time unmistakably possessed the favor of God and chased after His heart in a way that pleased Him. We are going to discover why God's favor rested on a sinful man.

David was not remarkable apart from God. God moved around him and through him in the most powerful stories. But something about the way David saw God transformed the way he lived. He saw God differently than everyone else around him. He loved God and he lived like he loved God. We are going to study the qualities David possessed as a result of what he believed about his God.

## What Pleases the Heart of God?

David began as a shepherd boy and became a king. God chose him, the youngest of his brothers, to be the king of Israel, and ultimately His eternal kingdom was realized through David's lineage in the birth of Jesus Christ.

We observe that David dealt more intimately with God, the Father, than any other person did in Scripture, except for Jesus Christ. David's personal prayers were recorded in the Psalms, and in them we get to see a relationship between a sinful man and a perfect God.

## What Is the Heart?

As Samuel is about to choose David as the next king, God reminds Samuel, "For the LORD sees not as man sees: man looks on the outward appearance, but the LORD looks on the **heart**" (1 Samuel 16:7, emphasis added). Throughout Scripture God seems to care more about the state of this unseen place in us, our hearts, rather than what everybody else can see in our behavior. While we judge each other by what we can see, God looks deep inside of us to see what nobody else sees. This is the place in us that holds what we love most . . . what we crave . . . what motivates us. This is the place that actually defines who we are.

Whether we acknowledge it or not, our lives are motivated by our hearts. So what we love determines how we live.

## Honest

My son, Conner, came home from fifth grade one day and told me his teacher was teaching him to pray like David. Curious what that meant, I asked, "How did David pray?" Conner said, "David didn't tell God what God wanted to hear, he told God what he was really feeling."

Today let's start there. Let's honestly bring our hearts to God and to each other. If any of you are like me, most of the time I don't have any idea how the deepest parts of me are doing. So just take a minute and pray before you move ahead. Ask God to give you insight to narrow down how you are doing right now.

## Project

Take a few minutes alone before God and answer these questions. Then come back together and discuss.

When your heart moves fast, what are you excited about?

When you feel disappointed or sad, what is it usually about?

When you feel content and most happy, what is it usually about?

What are the things you think about most?

For God to be pleased with you, what do you think you should be chasing?

Describe God. Answer as if He is one of your friends and you are telling someone about Him.

What is your heart chasing most?

Don't leave this first week with fear or guilt; we just need a starting place, enough honesty and self-awareness to know where we are beginning. If today you are just realizing your heart may be off-track, remember that God has known it well before today. And He is deeply pleased if you recognize it too.

*The LORD is near to all who call on him, to all who call on him in truth.*

## psalm 145:18

I pray these weeks would redefine the way you view God. I pray this time draws you into the most passionate relationship with your Creator. He is so ready to engage our souls.

# see ::

Watch video lesson 1:
GETTING STARTED: CHASE

Use streaming instructions
on inside cover or DVD.

Take notes if you like.

# ask ::

Use lesson 1: CHASE Conversation Cards for group discussion.

notes

# identity :: 2

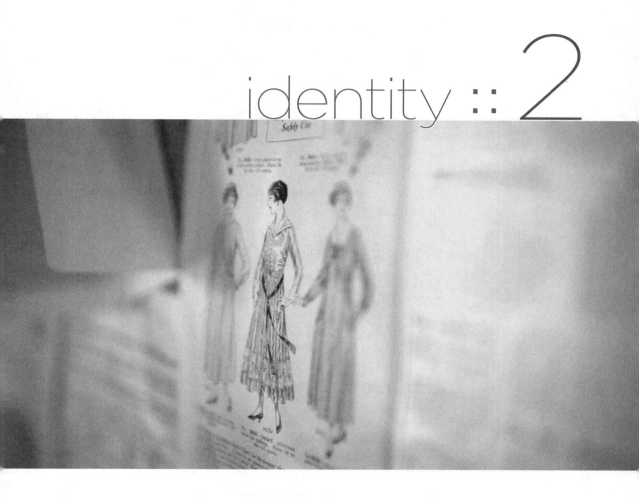

*The identity we are all chasing has already been given to us by God.*

Work through pages 32–47 on your own before your next group meeting and before you watch the next video teaching.

# What Is Identity?

Identity is found in the distinct characteristics that set us apart or give us worth.

We want to matter and to make a mark on the world. It feels selfish, even arrogant, to admit it. But every one of us has this need for a significant identity. This need possibly lies at the root of every human interaction and achievement. We all need to know why our life counts and what sets us apart, since life is short and there are a lot of us on this planet.

In the space below describe yourself. Who are you? What do you do? What is your personality like?

# Feet Down

I was innocently sitting in science class my sophomore year of high school, waiting for class to start, when two guys known for bullying turned around and decided it was the day to make me their target. I don't remember what they said, but I still can picture where I was sitting and what I was feeling. I felt like I was spinning and could not put my feet down. I could not land on what was true. As they laughed about who they perceived me to be, all I could think was,

"Who am I?"

I knew they did not know me and what they were saying was careless and untrue, but I did not know me and I did not know what was true. It wasn't long after that experience that I met God. And it wasn't until He began to undo me and define me that I finally could put my feet down and stop spinning. But even now, there are still plenty of days I spin, even with God in me.

No matter our age, we often find ourselves with feelings like those I had in high school. We have an identity crisis because we build our identity on things that move—things that aren't dependable or constant.

The list of what we build our identity on goes on and on:

family / bank accounts / friends / personality comfort / house / marriage / leadership / job vacations / children's success / relationships future / abilities / clothes / acceptance / love respect / morals / church / behavior / purpose

David lived a life unconcerned with appearances and image, rooted in a secure identity. Yet those of us who have put our faith in Christ live with the same identity; we just forget.

Let's begin this journey to discover where David's confidence and worth was rooted.

# study ::

read 1 samuel 16:1–13

# study

Even though very little is said about David's life directly in these verses, note some of the things we learn

about his life . . .

about his relationship to his father and brothers . . .

about where and how he likely spends his time . . .

about his heart . . .

about his new identity . . .

"And the Spirit of the LORD **rushed upon David from that day forward**" (1 Samuel 16:13, emphasis added). This single fact would go on to define every moment of the rest of this man's life, every psalm he would write and every obstacle he would overcome. What did it mean for David that the Spirit of God was on him?

Read these verses and consider how those of us who know Christ have a calling similar to David's.

_In him we have obtained an inheritance, having been predestined according to the purpose of him who works all things according to the counsel of his will, so that we who were the first to hope in Christ might be to the praise of his glory. In him you also, when you heard the word of truth, the gospel of your salvation, and believed in him, were sealed with the promised Holy Spirit, who is the guarantee of our inheritance until we acquire possession of it, to the praise of his glory._

## ephesians 1:11–14

**What does He say you are?**

**What does that mean to you?**

*But you are a chosen race, a royal priesthood, a holy nation, a people for his own possession, that you may proclaim the excellencies of him who called you out of darkness into his marvelous light. Once you were not a people, but now you are God's people; once you had not received mercy, but now you have received mercy.*

1 peter 2:9–10

**What does He say you are?**

**What does that mean to you?**

# Defining Myself

As long as we try to find our significance and worth in ourselves, we will feel disappointed. Self-esteem only works if we have a self worth esteeming. I am so sinful and selfish that I don't want to put my hope in myself.

Understanding these two truths keeps me from building my hope in myself:

1. We are all lost and pretty messed up, and
2. God in His grace rescued us.

As long as I am looking into myself for my identity, I will either be self-righteous about how great I am, which would be inaccurate, or distraught by the reality of the wreck I actually am.

The gospel steals all self-esteem:

---

*For I know that nothing good dwells in me, that is, in my flesh.*

romans 7:18

---

# Defined by God

"Nothing good" dwells in us. This statement in Romans is depressing if you don't hear the rest of the gospel. The whole story, the truth of the gospel, is we get something infinitely more sturdy and fulfilling than self-esteem. For those of us who know Christ, we stand on the unchanging reality that we have been so loved by our God that He purchased us with the blood of His Son. See, we have worth, but it doesn't come from within us—it comes to us from the One who made us. We share in a destiny and the calling David received that day. We have been rushed by the Spirit of God too. We will rule as sons and daughters of God someday. We have an insane calling, an insane identity.

*How great is the love the Father has lavished on us, that we should be called children of God! And that is what we are!*

## 1 john 3:1 NIV

If our true worth and significance and identity come from something so solid and eternal as God Himself, we don't have to pretend when we are imperfect. We don't stand on our accomplishments and personality and performance. We stand securely on the nature of an infinite, loving God. We don't have to manage our image or pretend we are okay, when we are really broken and imperfect. The grace God gives us in defining who we are changes everything.

## Uniquely Broken

---

*But we have this treasure in jars of clay, to show that the surpassing power belongs to God and not to us.*

2 corinthians 4:7

---

Christ's Spirit is this treasure inside of our broken lives, in us, moving and working in powerful and unique ways. Imperfect jars of clay each shaped uniquely to hold the Spirit of God for different purposes, each with unique marks and cracks and broken places. And through those spaces God shines out. The shameful places are torn down and become the places that are most useful to God.

The gospel strips us down to nothing but builds our hope in a secure, reckless, passionate God who loves us and saved us in spite of our messed-up selves. And then He uses those wrecked places to show His glory.

He is that good and, yes, we are that bad. All of us . . . especially those of us who think we aren't.

Our value comes from God; it can never be found in how we measure up. So whether you feel worthy or ashamed, this news should probably undo you. It is the character of God that gives us worth, not anything we have done or will do.

*For by grace you have been saved through faith. And this is not your own doing; it is the gift of God, not a result of works, so that no one may boast.*

ephesians 2:8–9

There is freedom in accepting our unworthiness and receiving God's worth. But self-esteem dies hard, especially for those of us who stand on a great performance.

The work of Christ steals all shame but it also steals all of our pride.

Who are you, Lord?  What do you want for me?

Read Psalm 23. In light of what you read, answer the questions above.

God desires for you to know His heart. He wants to lead you beside still waters and to restore your soul. He wants you to embrace your identity as His child. These are my hopes and prayers for you this week as you take time to reflect on His Word through these projects.

# be.

*Be still, and know that I am God. I will be exalted among the nations, I will be exalted in the earth!*

## psalm 46:10

It is hard to make the time and the space and to make our worlds quiet. We have to fight for it. It was in the quiet of the hills that an intimate relationship between David and God was born. It was when David was alone.

Get alone with God, with no agenda. Go outside and sit; turn off your phone. Pray and be with God. Confess your dependence. Thank Him. And listen.

> I lift up my eyes to the hills.
>     From where does my help come?
> My help comes from the Lord,
> who made heaven and earth.

psalm 121:1–2

*So then you are no longer strangers and aliens, but you are fellow citizens with the saints and members of the household of God, built on the foundation of the apostles and prophets, Christ Jesus himself being the cornerstone.*

## ephesians 2:19–20

# consider.

These blocks represent the things you have used to construct your identity. What have you built your identity around? On each block write something you have used to define yourself. (For example: kids, job, appearance, abilities, friends.)

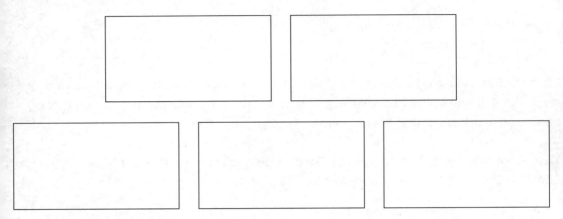

We all know these things are inadequate. But we are still building our lives and our worth on them.

How do you feel if the things you listed are threatened?

Who are you if you lose all of this?

# risk.

How much are you trying to control your image or what others think of you? Answer these questions:

Do you freely confess your current struggles to close friends?

When someone accuses you of something, do you immediately get defensive?

Are you quick to condemn when you hear about someone else screwing up? And do you feel like you are above making massive mistakes?

Do you get frantic when you feel misunderstood?

Do people think you have it all together?

There is freedom in understanding we are all equally and completely messed up, selfish, and prideful. We belittle the God of the universe whether we have an affair or we just worry He won't provide. None of us is above messing up, even in what some might consider small ways. We all have sinned and fallen short of God's glory. There is no way anyone can live as though they are better than someone else. God is our only hope, our Defender, our Definition, our Righteousness. Apart from Him there is no good thing.

# wrestle.

As we begin this journey, chasing the heart of God together, wrestle with what you know about God. Write a letter to Him—describe how you feel about Him right now. How do you feel when you approach Him to pray? How do you think He views you? Is His definition of you hard to believe?

Be honest. Put words to how you view Him and how you think He views you.

Dear God,

# Conclusion

The right answer is to rest our identity in the God who created us and defines us. He gives us our identity. The right answer sounds amazing and even potentially fulfilling. But most days it feels impossible to believe in an invisible kingdom, in an invisible God who actually loves us. So we attach ourselves and our worth to things we can see. We try to control our image, since what is inside feels impossible to fix.

This is the war that often consumes our lives; here lies the root of insecurity. But also on a good day when we feel our image is intact, there lies the root of pride. And neither insecurity nor pride serves as a fulfilling basis for our identity.

These questions matter, since they lie at the core of our hearts and navigate our lives.

## Who am I?

## How am I finding my identity in things outside of God? Is it working?

## How do I align my identity around God's character?

Do you want to know why David lived so confidently, so boldly? He actually believed this stuff. David believed God is who He says He is and what God said about him was true. David's God was real. David was God's and David knew it.

# see ::

Watch video lesson 2: IDENTITY

Use streaming instructions
on inside cover or DVD.

Take notes if you like.

# ask ::

Use lesson 2: IDENTITY
Conversation Cards for
group discussion.

# courage :: 3

*The fear of God makes people brave.*

Work through pages 54–69 on your own before your next group
meeting and before you watch the next video teaching.

*For God gave us a spirit not of fear but of power and love and self-control.*

**2 timothy 1:7**

## Seeing God

Fear has so captivated our minds we don't even recognize it anymore. It's just how we think. We live paralyzed, afraid to stand out yet also afraid of being invisible, afraid of something terrible happening yet also afraid something good will never happen. We live afraid of people and we think all of these thoughts are normal. We don't live seeing God, we live seeing worst-case scenarios.

While everyone stood around acting like they believed in God, David actually was experiencing Him. This is why God worked so powerfully through David's life. God was a matter of fact to David. God was so real, David found everyone else silly when they stood around not doing anything because they were afraid. He was recklessly brave simply because he knew God was real and with him.

Do we just confess an intellectual belief in God or is He real enough to impact our circumstances? Do we see God rather than physical realities? Fear is not just a little thing. Fear is stopping us from the things we are meant to be doing, the things God means for us to accomplish. And we must begin to experience God and hear Him or we will just stand there looking at whatever giants we face, unable to move forward. We need courage. But courage feels impossible to muster up on days we feel paralyzed by fear.

David wasn't especially courageous when he faced a giant; he just believed God was bigger than the man he faced. He believed God was real and with him. The same God with David is with us. God actually has plans for our days, and seeing God gives me the courage I need to live out His plans, no matter the risk.

> For this people's heart has grown dull,
>> and with their ears they can barely hear,
>> and their eyes they have closed;
> lest they should **see with their eyes**
>> and **hear with their ears**
> and **understand with their heart**
> and turn, and I would heal them.

acts 28:27, emphasis added

Do we see and hear God? Would we live in fear if we did?

Our fear of God has to expand to be greater than our fear of anything else. Fearing God simply means that, above any other thing, we love and want to please Him. The first of the Ten Commandments is, "You shall have no other gods before me" (Exodus 20:3). When God is in His right place, He will be the only thing we fear, the only thing we worship.

*Be willing to go out on a limb with Me. If that is where I am leading you, it is the safest place to be. . . . Your desire to live close to Me is at odds with your attempts to minimize risk. You are approaching a crossroads in your journey. In order to follow Me wholeheartedly, you must relinquish your tendency to play it safe.*

*Let Me lead you step by step through this day. If your primary focus is on Me, you can walk along perilous paths without being afraid. Eventually, you will learn to relax and enjoy the adventure of our journey together. As long as you stay close to Me, My sovereign Presence protects you wherever you go.*

**sarah young,** *Jesus Calling*[8]

8  Sarah Young, *Jesus Calling: Enjoying Peace in His Presence* (Nashville: Thomas Nelson, 2004), 360.

# study ::

read 1 samuel 17:1–51

What did the Israelite army believe about the situation, and how did they act upon their beliefs?

What was on the line if they fought?

What did David believe about the situation, and how did he act upon his beliefs?

How was David different from every other man there? What gave him the courage to act?

What was David's motive for fighting Goliath? What did he want most?

# Nothing to Lose

The smaller this life gets and the bigger God and the next life get, the more we are willing to risk here on this earth. We live courageously because in light of God's glory, we don't have as much to lose. Courage is grounded in a big view of God.

A truly dangerous person is one who has nothing to lose. Saul and all of the Israelite men were protective of themselves, their freedom, their comfortable lives. David did not see what he might lose, he saw God; he saw God's glory and name being mocked, and in faith he was motivated to bring glory to God. David did not live protectively of this life; he had nothing to lose here, because he believed his God was real and heaven was coming.

Fear is rooted in unbelief and unbelief is sin. Courage is fundamentally a fight for faith. We fight to believe all the way down to the deepest parts of us that God is real and enough. He alone makes us brave.

# Romans 8

*For all who are led by the Spirit of God are sons of God. For you did not receive the spirit of slavery to fall back into fear, but you have received the Spirit of adoption as sons, by whom we cry, "Abba! Father!"*

romans 8:14–15

Why does Romans say we don't have to fall back into fear?

How does God being your loving Father inspire courage?

# Courage in the Everyday

*One who is faithful in a very little is also faithful in much.*

## luke 16:10a

Courage is grown in the mundane, small pieces of our lives.

So what does it look like to bravely follow God in the small things?
:: Ask the cashier how she is and listen as she responds.

:: Deal with unresolved conflicts at work, in your family, with your friends.

:: Make friends at the park or in your dorm or at your office.

:: Forgive the friend who keeps hurting you.

:: Serve your church in a way no one sees.

:: Be intentional with time you have with your kids or your friends. Be present.

::  Make the most of every opportunity to respond to need,
    whether it is the homeless man on the side of the road or your
    grandparents who need a visit.

Every day wake up and live fully for God's glory. These are some
suggestions, but where is God calling you to live more bravely in
the everyday?

## Courage in the Impossible

Something about our position as God's children should eradicate
our fear. We should not live in a paralyzed state, because there is
power in understanding our Father, God. He is enough and He sees
us. So whether our Goliath is a move overseas to serve unreached
people or facing a new diagnosis of cancer, God is with us and He
will not forsake us.

Last night I sat in my car with a dear friend whose husband recently
moved out. She is the mother of four young kids. Fear flooded the
car as we sat considering her future.

There are never words in moments like this. I grabbed her arms and said, "God sees you. He sees your kids. He is real and alive and pressing into this, even though it feels like He turned His head for a moment. He didn't turn His head. He is here." Then we talked to Him. There in the driveway, outside of little bedrooms with little hurting people and big unknown futures, we talked to an invisible God.

And in that moment we remembered that He was real and coming and that today He would be enough to face the scariest things. We don't face this life alone. He is behind us in all things. Do we see Him?

When David was a child, tending his sheep and obeying God, when no one saw him in the fields, he was building a story of faith. When the time came for him to face his giant, David feared God on that impossible day because he had learned to fear God in the everyday. Courage for the impossible is most often built by God growing our faith in Him in the everyday. We live by faith, not by sight.

Who are you, Lord?  What do you want for me?

Read Psalm 27. In light of what you read, answer the questions above.

As you approach your time with God this week, pray He will expose the strongholds that keep you from recklessly following Him.

# consider.

Consider these three verses before answering the questions that follow:

*Then Samuel took the horn of oil and anointed him in the midst of his brothers. And the Spirit of the LORD rushed upon David from that day forward. And Samuel rose up and went to Ramah.*

## 1 samuel 16:13

*For God gave us a spirit not of fear but of power and love and self-control.*

## 2 timothy 1:7

*But you will receive power when the Holy Spirit has come upon you, and you will be my witnesses in Jerusalem and in all Judea and Samaria, and to the end of the earth.*

## acts 1:8

Compare the power given to David with the power given to those who believe in Christ.

Why do we limit the Holy Spirit's voice and power in our lives?

*Since we have the same spirit of faith according to what has been written, "I believed, and so I spoke," we also believe, and so we also speak.*

## 2 corinthians 4:13

# ask.

Pray and ask God what He is calling you to do, to say, or to be that you have not previously considered because of fear or a hard heart.

Write down the things that are brought to mind or pressed on your heart.

_____

_____

_____

_____

_____

_____

_____

_____

*For this people's heart has grown dull, and with their ears they can barely hear, and their eyes they have closed.*

## acts 28:27a

_____

# imagine.

Imagine what it would look like if you lived out a childlike, reckless, and courageous faith like David had in 1 Samuel 17. Draw what comes to mind.

<br>
<br>
<br>
<br>
<br>
<br>
<br>
<br>

What is keeping you from living out that kind of faith?

Who or what is your "Goliath"?

Who or what causes you to feel insecurity and doubt as David's brother did in 1 Samuel 17:28?

# commit.

Write your own psalm (prayer) and consider including some of these things:

:: Describe and praise God for who you know Him to be.

:: Ask for forgiveness for not hearing or seeing the call and power of God.

:: Confess ways you have not believed God.

:: Commit to obeying God in the ways He is calling you to walk courageously.

_____

_____

_____

_____

_____

_____

_____

_____

_____

_____

_____

_____

_____

_____

_____

# Conclusion

What if we became insanely courageous and began to live the stories God has written for us?

What if we could truly love people without fear of how they would receive us?

What if we could give without needing anything in return?

What if we actually began living our dreams instead of squashing them back into safer places?

I believe God is calling us to a life like this, but not in our own strength. He wants us to see that He is able. He is for us. He is our hope and we live this out for His glory. We were made for that. We were made to display the glory of our Creator through our lives, through our freedom from fear. Fearing and loving God alone makes every other fear disappear.

# see ::

Watch video lesson 3: COURAGE

Use streaming instructions
on inside cover or DVD.

Take notes if you like.

# ask ::

Use lesson 3: COURAGE
Conversation Cards for
group discussion.

# obedience :: 4

*The more we trust God, the more we obey Him.*

Work through pages 76–92 on your own before your next group
meeting and before you watch the next video teaching.

For you bless the righteous, O LORD;
you cover him with favor as with a shield.

psalm 5:12

# Teenage Rebellion

I remember the sound my heart made. It was pounding so hard, so loud, fighting against my efforts to stay calm, I thought it may win and beat me down. Sitting on the floor of our room in the sorority house with my best friend, Kathryn, we had been praying and both of us couldn't shake the feeling we needed to pray for our friend Sarah. So we did. Sarah may have been the most confident and admired girl in our sorority, and after we finished praying we knew we were supposed to talk to her about God. I had known Sarah since middle school and never once talked to her about God. But I was learning to trust the leadings God was putting in me. Still, as Kathryn and I headed down the stairs to find her, I couldn't help whispering to myself, "I hope she is not here," and "God, I'll obey, but you'd better show up."

When Sarah got to her room, Kathryn and I were waiting for her and, certain we were about to look so foolish, we awkwardly told her we had been praying and now we were going to tell her about God. I kind-of butchered the whole thing. But immediately she started crying, and she sat down on our floor without a moment's hesitation and eagerly waited to hear what we had to say. It may have been one of the most beautiful things I have ever seen. Sarah was hurting for God and God sent us awkwardly to get her.

It was one time I obeyed the odd and small leading of God. How many other times I have not and how many beautiful moments I'm sure I have missed.

Most of my life something rebellious has risen up in me when I hear the word *obey*. I'd turn into a toddler, or maybe more like a teenager, who knows what is right and just doesn't want to do it. I learned as a child that my behavior mattered more than my heart. My parents were certainly not the only culprits for teaching me this; school, church, friends, and jobs all taught me this. So naturally the feelings of pressure that accompany such an upbringing make me cringe when I hear words like *obey* or *submit*. And naturally all of that eventually carried over to my relationship with God.

However, God began to transform my view of Him in college, and as my view of Him grew, my trust in Him grew and my obedience to Him grew, not out of fear but because I wanted Him more than my own way. I wanted Him more than my friends' approval. So on nights spent on floors, praying, when He told me to do awkward, foolish things, I actually did them.

When I read the stories you are going to read below, I am convicted, and I desperately want to be like David, not Saul. Saul was the king prior to David, but he lost God's blessing on the day described in these verses. It was not because of his behavior; it was because of his heart. This is a key point because, as we will see later in this study, some of the sin David will commit is heinous too. So if the issue is not that Saul sinned more than David, what, then, is the issue?

Compare David's and Saul's hearts in these two similar battles. What were the differences in these two men?

# study ::
## saul

read 1 samuel 15:1-31

What did God ask of Saul?

How did Saul disobey?

What motivated Saul to disobey?

What was God's response?

What was it about Saul's heart that displeased God?

# study ::
## david

## read 1 samuel 23:2-14

What did God ask of David?

How did David respond?

What do you think motivated David to obey?

What was God's response?

What was it about David's heart that pleased God?

Look at these two lists of motivations that drove Saul and David. Think about your life and what motives are driving you.

| Saul | David | Your Motivations |
|------|-------|------------------|
| Practical wisdom | Reckless obedience | _____ |
| People's approval | God's opinion | _____ |
| Self-provision | God's provision | _____ |
| Recognition | God's approval | _____ |
| Immediate reward | Other people's welfare | _____ |
| Power | Dependence | _____ |
| Self-protection | God's protection | _____ |

David trusted God. He trusted God's character, unlike Saul and unlike Adam and Eve. Adam and Eve disobeyed because they thought God was holding out on them. They did not trust God. Trust in the character of God is foundational to obedience.

# Following the Rules

Many of us hear the word *obedience* and based on past experiences we feel pressure, and words like *rules*, *punishment*, and *shame* come to mind. Deep in the crevasses of present-day Christendom lies the backward theology that good behavior pleases God. But morality—doing good things for the sake of doing good things—has never won God's favor. As we'll see later, David's life was far from moral. David became tangled in adultery and even murder. He was not moral, yet he was considered right before God.

It's not that Saul sinned more than David. So why was Saul rejected by God and David accepted? Something about the invisible places within each of the men was fundamentally different toward God.

---

*We know that a person is not justified by works of the law but through faith in Jesus Christ, so we also have believed in Christ Jesus, in order to be justified by faith in Christ and not by works of the law, because by works of the law no one will be justified.*

## galatians 2:16

---

Morality is something we achieve, while righteousness is something we receive. God makes us right because of Jesus, and our love and obedience to Him is empowered and accomplished through Christ.

As good and miraculous as this is, our pride doesn't want it to be true. We want to be good enough on our own.

Faith in God has always been and will always be what makes us right before God.

Faith = Righteousness that comes from Christ = God's acceptance

---

*For it is by grace you have been saved, through faith—and this is not from yourselves . . .*

**ephesians 2:8** NIV

---

# Belittling God

At some point Saul quit trusting God. He started caring more about pleasing the people around him than obeying God, and he did not see his sin as a big deal. I am constantly guilty of the same thing. The sins I can hide become acceptable and so I accept them. I tuck them back where no one sees and I let them grow. Then I am surprised when I feel sick from chasing everything I knew would make my insides hurt. The reality is I would rather have a day full of all my favorite things than a moment of tasting God. I belittle God and the offense is so great because I offend Someone so great.

We all lack faith and belittle God regularly. We are no better than Saul; we are pleasing men instead of God. But do we really see how sinful we are before our good and holy God?

John Piper says the mark of a believer is not the absence of sin but the fact that we are fighting sin.[9] We should feel uncomfortable with our sin because it offends our God. But when confronted with his sin, Saul did not repent, he begged God to save his reputation. Saul's relationship with his people was more important to him than his relationship with God, and he justified his sinful actions by claiming he had good intentions.

Most of us, if we are honest, have been there. Like Saul, we sin against God but explain our reasons so beautifully that everyone but God pats us on the back. Or in some cases, we might avoid sin at all costs, but our lack of sin is motivated by what others think of us; it has little or nothing to do with God.

God simply asks us for our obedience and our trust. What was so beautiful and unique about David was his deep affection for God and his desire to obey Him no matter what it meant for his time on earth and no matter what anyone else thought.

9   John Piper, *Future Grace* (Colorado Springs: Multnomah, 2005), 329.

Who are you, Lord?  What do you want for me?

Read Psalm 63. In light of what you read, answer the questions above.

Why is it difficult for us to obey? My hope for you as you approach these projects is that you will identify some of the things keeping you from experiencing the blessing of obedience.

# reflect.

Look at your own heart in light of Saul's.

_____

*Saul said to Samuel, "I have sinned, for I have transgressed the commandment of the LORD and your words, because I feared the people and obeyed their voice."*

## 1 samuel 15:24

_____

Has your fear of people become greater than your fear of God?

If yes, give some examples.

Respond to God about this struggle in your life.

# compare.

Check out these verses:

> For you will not delight in sacrifice, or I would give it;
>> you will not be pleased with a burnt offering.
> The sacrifices of God are a broken spirit;
>> a broken and contrite heart, O God, you will not despise.
>
> psalm 51:16–17

---

*For in it the righteousness of God is revealed from faith for faith, as it is written, "The righteous shall live by faith."*

**romans 1:17**

---

*And he believed the LORD, and he counted it to him as righteousness.*

**genesis 15:6**

---

*And without faith it is impossible to please him, for whoever would draw near to God must believe that he exists and that he rewards those who seek him.*

**hebrews 11:6**

---

What do you believe is the difference between morality and true righteousness? Write the qualities of each below. List the different qualities between morality and true righteousness.

Morality

_____

_____

_____

_____

_____

_____

_____

_____

_____

_____

True Righteousness

_____

_____

_____

_____

_____

_____

_____

_____

_____

_____

On most days what do you feel like it is God wants from you?

What do you think He actually wants from you?

# rewind.

*And because you are sons, God has sent the Spirit of his Son into our hearts, crying, "Abba! Father!"*

## galatians 4:6

Oftentimes our view of obedience and even our view of God come from our relationship with our earthly father. Explore how this earthly relationship is affecting your relationship with God.

If you had a father in your life growing up, write about what he expected from you as a child.

Did you measure up to those expectations?

How has that impacted the way you relate to God?

# imagine.

If God were your physical Father on earth, describe what kind of Father you think He would be.

What would He do with you?

What would He hope for you?

What would He expect from you?

What would your conversations be about?

# Conclusion

There are so many reasons we cringe when we hear words like *obedience* and *submission*:

:: We don't believe God asks us to obey for our own good.

:: We don't believe God truly cares for us.

:: We don't believe God knows everything.

:: We want to be our own captains.

:: We want to control our own lives.

I am a parent now and I see all of these same struggles in my kids. Learning to trust God is a lot like a child learning to trust a father. It takes time and a genuine relationship.

## Do you trust that God's desires for you are good?

## Do you think you control your life better than He does?

Relationships are always built on trust and trust leads to obedience.

# see ::

Watch video lesson 4: OBEDIENCE

Use streaming instructions
on inside cover or DVD.

Take notes if you like.

# ask ::

Use lesson 4: OBEDIENCE
Conversation Cards for
group discussion.

belief :: 5

*How we live every second of every day will flow
out of what we believe about God.*

Work through pages 100–114 on your own before your next group
meeting and before you watch the next video teaching.

# Promise Me

Recently, my good friend Amanda pulled together a room full of neighbors to do a Bible study. Most of the room wasn't sure what they believed about God. I was given a few minutes to teach about God and grace, and when I did, Colleen, who sat closest to me, stopped me and said, "I find it hard to believe we don't have to do anything to measure up to God. It sounds good, but I just can't believe that."

I sometimes doubt too. Every once in a while the thought will go through my mind,

"What if there is no God?"

Heaven and angels and hell and God in heaven and Christ raised from the dead . . . it's easy to question, and in those moments my soul feels dark. It's as if I've just been yanked out of the most comfortable, beautiful home and I'm left in a dark alley, alone with nothing. In that moment I taste hopelessness.

After the thought passes and I remember the undeniable presence of God everywhere in my life, even in every piece of creation, peace and hope flood me again. If we are honest, there are moments or seasons we all doubt, because every foundational thing about us depends on invisible stuff.

I stand on the promise that I will live for eternity as a child of God (Romans 8:15), that God will work all things together for good because I love Him (Romans 8:28), and that He lives in me and is a very present help in struggles (Psalm 46:1). I trust He prepared good works for me to do in advance and I just have to look to Him and He will carry them out (Ephesians 2:10). I stand on the promise that He formed me in my mother's womb and knows my every thought (Psalm 139:13).

These promises are so deep within me, they are holding me up and driving me. These promises are made even more beautiful because they are not hinging on some spectacular performance from me while I am here on earth. God promises these things and I am just a recipient. But do we really believe all of this invisible stuff?

**How often do we doubt God in some form or fashion?**

Daily.

Doubt is the root of all sin. I know we all doubt Him, because if we fully believed God every moment, we would all be living radical, completely sold-out lives. I think David's incredible God-filled life was evidence of just that.

*Jesus said to him, "Have you believed because you have seen me? Blessed are those who have not seen and yet have believed."*

## john 20:29

God promised David things that would lay the foundation for all of the promises we stand on today.

# study ::

## read 2 samuel 7:1-17

(Note: These verses point to Jesus, but verse 14 is talking about Solomon.)

What is the overarching promise God made to David?

## Fulfilled Promises

This enormous promise of an eternal kingdom that God makes to David is a beautiful promise and we get to be a part of it through Christ. We are blessed to be on this side of the cross, looking back on the redeeming work of Christ rather than waiting in expectation of it. The hope of the world has always been and always will be Jesus Christ.

---

*And behold, you will conceive in your womb and bear a son, and you shall call his name Jesus. He will be great and will be called the Son of the Most High. And the Lord God will give to him the throne of his father David, and he will reign over the house of Jacob forever, and of his kingdom there will be no end.*

luke 1:31–33

---

*I, Jesus, have sent my angel to testify to you about these things for the churches. I am the root and the descendant of David, the bright morning star.*

**revelation 22:16**

Write about how the promises God made to David affect you today.

Read David's response to God's promises.

---

*Then King David went in and sat before the LORD and said, "Who am I, O Lord GOD, and what is my house, that you have brought me thus far? And yet this was a small thing in your eyes, O Lord GOD. . . . And what more can David say to you? For you know your servant, O Lord GOD! . . . Now therefore may it please you to bless the house of your servant, so that it may continue forever before you. For you, O Lord GOD, have spoken, and with your blessing shall the house of your servant be blessed forever."*

## 2 samuel 7:18–19, 20, 29

---

## Put yourself in David's position. How did these promises change his life?

## How did these promises change his relationship with God?

*And have mercy on those who doubt.*

jude 1:22

## Questioning

I was eighteen, sitting on the bed of my dorm room reading the cries of David, this mess of a man, in the Psalms. As I read, it was as if God were telling me,

*Stop, Jennie. Stop pretending. Stop playing nice.*

These words wrecked me and I wondered if I really was safe enough to talk to God this way. But I was tired of pretending. So I got in my car and started driving, playing music loud enough to cover the sounds of my yelling. I yelled at God for the first time in my life. He was supposed to bless me because I was serving Him. And yet I couldn't get the approval I was longing for from friends, from family. I could not reconcile unresolved hurts from my past and I could not understand how God could have allowed those hurts to happen. My life was still not working. I was moral and I thought God owed me something for it. I thought He owed me happiness.

study

I finished yelling at God. By this point I had driven far out of the city. I came to a pond and I got out and knelt on the ground, and there in the quiet after the first fight I had with God . . .

He was there. He fell into my questions in the most brilliant way I had ever seen or felt before. He fell into the space in me I thought would push Him further away. He fell into the places I had sinned against Him. He met me in my anger and reminded me of His great unwavering love for me. I was His and nothing I felt, no matter how wrong, could shake Him from me. And in that night He was enough for me; His approval felt better than the elusive compliments I had been chasing from people, and in trusting Him with my hurt and disappointment, I found Him in it with me. He didn't feel like my enemy anymore. My God was real and He loved me despite my sense of entitlement, my doubts, and my pride. It is one of my favorite and most intimate moments I have ever had with God.

God can handle our doubts. He is big enough. But we have got to quit pretending faith is easy. We fight for faith and ask God to give it.

*And Lord, haste the day when my faith shall be sight,*
*The clouds be rolled back as a scroll;*
*The trump shall resound, and the Lord shall descend,*
*Even so, it is well with my soul.*
*It is well, with my soul,*
*It is well, with my soul,*
*It is well, it is well, with my soul.*

**horatio spafford, "It Is Well With My Soul"**

## Respond

As God made a promise in 2 Samuel 7 to David, He was revealing His plan for salvation. Throughout the Psalms David was overwhelmed by the protection and salvation he received from the Lord. We have the same story as David, the promise of participating in a kingdom that lasts forever, because of Christ. Read as David reflects on the covenant God has made with him.

# Who are you, Lord? & What do you want for me?

Read Psalm 110. In light of what you read, answer the questions above.

As you spend time with the Lord this week, wrestle through your faith. What is your faith built upon?

# wrestle.

Be completely honest. What are the areas of your faith you find yourself doubting most often? Write them in the "Doubts" section below.

**Doubts**

**Scripture**

_____    _____

_____    _____

_____    _____

_____    _____

_____    _____

_____    _____

_____    _____

Now look up scripture concerning each doubt you feel and write out God's truth in the "Scripture" section beside each doubt you listed. This Web site may prove helpful in your search: http://www.biblegateway.com/.

_____

*Take care, brothers, lest there be in any of you an evil, unbelieving heart, leading you to fall away from the living God.*

## hebrews 3:12

_____

# reflect.

Describe a time in your life when, beyond a shadow of a doubt, God was real to you.

. . . a time when something happened that was beyond coincidence.

. . . a time that gave you confidence that there is an Author to our lives.

The word *remember* is found in Scripture over 150 times.[10] It's not every day in our lives we have a mountaintop experience with God. He wants to assure us our faith is real through our memories of the times when it was undoubtedly real and through the promises of His Word.

But unfortunately we forget. Come back to this page whenever you are having doubts, and remember again the times when He was most real to you.

10  http://www.twopaths.com/faq_wordcount.htm

# imagine.

If you met God today, imagine what you would talk about. What would you ask Him?

What would you celebrate with Him?

What would you wish you had done differently?

What would it feel like to see all you have believed become a visible reality?

The day you meet God face-to-face will one day be a reality. Are you living like it will be?

---

*And no longer shall each one teach his neighbor and each his brother, saying, "Know the LORD," for they shall all know me, from the least of them to the greatest, declares the LORD. For I will forgive their iniquity, and I will remember their sin no more.*

## jeremiah 31:34

---

# commit.

What are the areas in which you continue to doubt God, His provision, or His goodness?

On this side of the line
write the areas you doubt.

---

On this side of the line
write your prayer to Him,
asking Him for more faith
in these areas.

Note: Sometimes you can't and shouldn't quit wrestling with God. Some doubts need more than a few scriptures to comfort. But you can commit to dealing with your doubt through counseling, personal study, and prayer. Just don't walk away from studying this week until you have a plan to hash these things out with God.

# Conclusion

I think of my kids and how right answers on their lips do not move me, the perfectly combed hair and put-together table manners do not move me. But my child looking at me, confused about the evil and suffering he just observed, or my child wondering why she did not make it when she did her absolute best, or my child crying as I have to punish him and it just hurts . . . then I am moved—moved to hold, to love, to restore, to comfort, to be.

So often as believers we are afraid to question God.

*Question*. And don't apologize.

As if He can't handle our doubt or questions or hurt or disappointment. As if He wanted happy robots. We are how He made us: weak and needy, confused and complicated and in need of God, especially a God we can't understand.

I need a God whom I cannot understand. I need a God big enough to have purposes for my life that are beyond what I can see. And because He happens to be that big and purposeful, our shallow, small hearts will question.

And that big God will move; He'll move toward me to hold, to love, to restore, to comfort, to be. And I would never want to miss that.

# see ::

Watch video lesson 5: BELIEF

Use streaming instructions
on inside cover or DVD.

Take notes if you like.

# ask ::

Use lesson 5: BELIEF Conversation
Cards for group discussion.

# repentance :: 6

*It is God's mercy to show us our sin and lead us to repentance.*

Work through pages 122–134 on your own before your next group meeting and before you watch the next video teaching.

# Hiding or Running

I couldn't find Kate. We were all home after our Easter church service, grandparents and other family seated at the table and ready to eat. I had left Kate in my room after having to punish her. Kate, who was seven years old at the time, rarely gets in trouble; she is a joyful, easy kid. After she had come to understand what she had done wrong and had served her time-out, I expected to find her drying her tears, wiping her nose, and preparing to join us. But she was nowhere to be found. I called loudly for her and even went around the outside of the house once. I came back into my room and heard sniffles coming from my closet. I opened the door and could hear her crying but couldn't see her.

I got on my hands and knees and there she was under all my hanging clothes, arms and legs mixed in with sandals and boots. She was overwhelmed with shame and couldn't face anyone, so she hid. She thought she had lost me; she thought she had forever messed everything up.

Like Kate, we all mess up, even after God has done so much for us. Guilt and shame sink into the holes of our failures and we either run from those feelings or they paralyze us.

But whether we are ignoring our sin or sitting in the junk of it on a closet floor, we all feel shame. Some of us just cope with that feeling better than others. We like to mask our weakness till we find ourselves believing we're all right.

It is trouble to feel broken. It is trouble to need God.

There are two places we typically run when we see our sin.

1.  We hide like Adam and Eve, making fig leaves . . . we hide in our closets under clothes of religion or morality.

2.  We run from God in outright rebellion like the prodigal son.

Both responses take us further from freedom, further from God's love.

Repentance is the confession of the specific ways I have offended God, turning away from that sin and toward God for forgiveness. God doesn't ask us to confess our sin so we will feel guilty. He asks us to confess our sin to find freedom and to come back to Him.

---

*He who conceals his sins does not prosper, but whoever confesses and renounces them finds mercy.*

**proverbs 28:13** NIV

---

David sinned in some big ways, as we are going to study, and when God showed him his sin, he didn't hide and he didn't run. He fell before God. Something about coming to the end of ourselves, when we can't pretend we are good anymore, shows us just how much we always needed God. Seeing our great need for God leads us back to Him.

# study ::

read 2 samuel 11
and
2 samuel 12:1–14

What were David's sins?


How did God choose to convict David of his
sin?


What was David's response to God after he was
convicted?

---

*Those who are well have no need of a physician, but those who are sick. I came not to call the
righteous, but sinners.*

## mark 2:17

---

*But God chose what is foolish in the world to shame the wise; God chose what is weak in the world
to shame the strong.*

## 1 corinthians 1:27

---

*But he said to me, "My grace is sufficient for you, for my power is made perfect in weakness." Therefore I will boast all the more gladly of my weaknesses, so that the power of Christ may rest upon me.*

**2 corinthians 12:9**

---

Use the scales below to think about your own level of conviction.

Do you live in need of God?

1------2------3------4------5------6------7------8------9-----10

I don't live like
I need God

I live in great
need of God

Do you live with an awareness of your sin?

1------2------3------4------5------6------7------8------9-----10

I don't believe
I sin often

I am aware of my
constant sinfulness

Do you grieve the ways you have offended God?

1------2------3------4------5------6------7------8------9-----10
I do not grieve my                                          I am grieved
offenses                                                    by my sin

The goal of repentance is not to air out our junk. The goal and
beauty of repentance is that it restores our relationship with God.
When we acknowledge our sin, we state what God already knows,
and we state that we need Him to make us right. Pride is destroyed
with transparent repentance.

David could not stand the sin of a man taking a lamb, while he
himself had murdered a man and taken his wife. Wasn't this human
of him? We all do this: we see the sin of others so clearly but can't
seem to remember how we have offended God.

Repentance is painful because none of us want to admit how far we
are from good.

A contrite heart pleases God, a heart that sees its need for a Savior.

> The sacrifices of God are a broken spirit;
>     a broken and **contrite** heart, O God, you will not
>     despise.
>
> psalm 51:17, emphasis added

God doesn't despise remorseful hearts, because He can work them. On the following pages you are going to glimpse into one of the most brutal, passionate journal entries ever. Our hope to be rescued from our sin is never hope in itself; it is hope in the character of God. God is the One who delivers, restores, and cleans. He alone is able to save.

## Respond

This Psalm is an intense glimpse into the heart of this broken man, David. As you read the Psalm, respond to the questions on the next page.

# study

Who are you, Lord?  What do you want for me?

Read Psalm 32. In light of what you read, answer the questions above.

As you approach God in study this week, my hope is you will come with a broken and contrite heart. Some of you feel broken to the point of shame. I pray you will find rest in the freedom of God's encompassing grace.

# consider.

In what areas do you need to experience God's forgiveness?

Are there any sins you are holding onto that are causing you shame? Name them.

From what we have studied this week, what do you think God would say to you concerning your shame?

*To the Lord our God belong mercy and forgiveness, for we have rebelled against him.*

**daniel 9:9**

# discover.

*Therefore do not pronounce judgment before the time, before the Lord comes, who will bring to light the things now hidden in darkness and will disclose the purposes of the heart.*

## 1 corinthians 4:5

God knows our hearts. We are unable to hide from Him. Spend some time alone with God. Journal to Him, confessing your hidden sin, motives, agendas, and pride.

Dear God,

# imagine.

As you have studied this week, how have you come to think God wants you to relate to Him? What is He chasing after in you?

Draw a picture of what you feel God is looking for in you. Use an analogy or an image that represents the concept.

# deal.

Grab one or two friends who know you well and love you, and take them to dinner or coffee. (If you don't have people like this right now, start praying for God to bring them into your life.) Ask them to be "Nathans" in your life—to be truth tellers. Talk about your blind spots, sin struggles, and weaknesses. Ask them to be honest and do not defend yourself. Also talk honestly about your gifts and strengths. This will be difficult but it could also be life-changing. Afterward, journal about your experience.

People see our junk. We need to be aware of it too.

> Iron sharpens iron,
>     and one man sharpens another.

proverbs 27:17

# Conclusion

Against you, you only, have I sinned
  and done what is evil in your sight.

psalm 51:4

Unless we find ourselves in the words of Psalm 51:4, we are unaware of our sin. Our limited view of sin usually involves us carrying around rulers, measuring ourselves and our sins against others. Some of us feel hopeless because our sin feels even worse than David's. But others of us believe we are okay because we just aren't that bad.

God's view of sin encompasses any unbelief, anything short of loving God with your entire mind, soul, and strength, which is the greatest commandment. Belittling Him in any way is as offensive to Him as murder or adultery, because the sin is against our holy God and Creator. As I've pointed out before, the sin is so great because we sin against Someone so great. Every single one of us does this, every single day. It's one thing to say we sin, though, and it's another thing to actually enter into the reality of that dark moment to feel the weight and sadness of what sin truly means for us.

But after the dark moments God steps in to save us despite our wreck of a life. Digging up sin is about as fun as digging up concrete, but it is necessary and worth it. To taste the forgiveness and freedom God offers is the sweetest thing this side of heaven. Grace gets real when we see our need for it.

# see ::

Watch video lesson 6:
REPENTANCE

Use streaming instructions
on inside cover or DVD.

Take notes if you like.

# ask ::

Use lesson 6: REPENTANCE
Conversation Cards for
group discussion.

# surrender :: 7

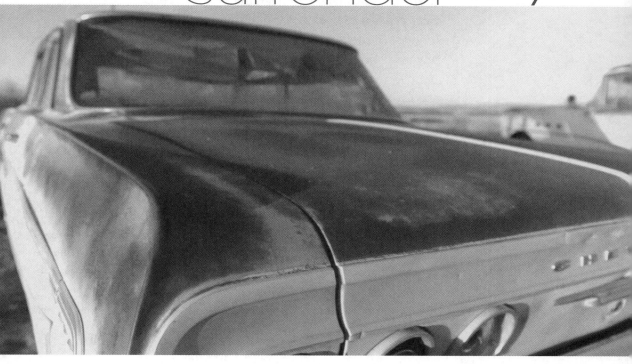

*Surrender to God is not dictated by our circumstances.*

Work through pages 142–154 on your own before your next group meeting and before you watch the next video teaching.

# Pretty Expectations

My sister Brooke had been through so much in such a short amount of time it physically hurt to think of it. Months before it all, we had walked on the beach together, analyzing how we, now in our thirties, had come so far from the entitled attitudes we carried post-college. Life was no longer made up of boxes to check on a long list of pretty expectations. We were over it. Life wasn't perfect anymore, but now more than we wanted perfection and being happy, we wanted God. But to get God we were learning to receive our lives rather than try to control them. With sand in our toes and a healthy baby girl growing in Brooke's tummy, these were the topics of our day: a God who could not be controlled, and how much we wanted more of Him. It was a beautiful day and an even more beautiful conversation.

Two months later, baby Lucy would be born to my sister and her husband in the middle of the night, already with Jesus. Nights you hold babies that don't breathe make you wonder if God is real. He seemed harder to spot in that dark hospital room than beside the waves on that bright day when my sister and I walked together. Even though we had meant every word by the ocean, we wanted to take them back that night.

*God, we want to control our lives, because You don't feel safe enough.*

Somewhere along the way I picked up the idea that if I loved God,
He was supposed to bless me . . . in spite of every piece of evidence
to the contrary. Death, sickness, divorce, infertility, and depression
seem to not take into account the spiritual lives of their victims.
Often it is the people I respect most who seem to be suffering the
most. So it begs the question . . .

**Are we willing to surrender fully to a God who may let us suffer?**

---

*And he said . . .* "The LORD gave, and the LORD has taken away; blessed be the name
of the LORD."

# job 1:21, emphasis added

---

As we approach this sensitive subject, you will see God's call on
David's life did not prevent him from suffering. The last seasons of
David's life were filled with unfathomable hurt.

# study ::

read 2 samuel 13

and

2 samuel 18:13–33

Describe the major events David saw unfold in his children's lives.

Describe what David could have been thinking and feeling.

What would you have been thinking if you had spent your life serving God and suddenly your life began to fall apart?

Jesus never promises there won't be trouble. He promises to be our peace through it.

*I have told you these things, so that in me you may have peace. In this world you will have trouble. But take heart! I have overcome the world.*

## john 16:33 NIV

We have to lay down the false sense of entitlement we have built that God owes us a good life. Jesus was clear about what to expect here: "In this world you WILL have trouble."

# Getting God

Throughout Scripture God confirms what anyone who lives on this planet should already know: that all people, even good people, suffer. The primary reason most of us live in disappointment is that we have put our hope in this life and, not surprisingly, it has failed us. Our one and only sustaining hope is that God has overcome this world and is preparing our home in the next. We certainly experience God's blessings in this life, but blessings are not promises.

Honestly, we also live in disappointment because we are not that impressed with the fact that as believers in Christ, we get God. We think He is not enough for us. We want more. Pull back from these temporary days here on earth and consider that we aren't here long. Paul says, "I consider everything [even my gains] a loss compared to the surpassing greatness of knowing Christ Jesus my Lord" (Philippians 3:8 NIV). Oh to view Christ this way, with this affection. For Paul, nothing here on earth could compare to knowing Christ.

Nothing good on this earth even compares to God's love, and no suffering compares to the suffering of being separated from God. Every human living on earth experiences common grace, the everyday participation of God in creation: the sun and the stars, and laughter and hope and babies, and coffee and gifts and fulfillment, and on and on. To truly be forsaken by God would be the definition of suffering. Those of us who have been saved by Christ will never taste this kind of suffering, because Christ faced God's wrath for us.

> He was despised and rejected by men,
>    a man of sorrows, and familiar with suffering. . . .
> Surely he took up our infirmities
>    and carried our sorrows,
> yet we considered Him stricken by God,
>    smitten by him, and afflicted.
> But he was pierced for our transgressions,
>    he was crushed for our iniquities.

isaiah 53:3, 4–5 NIV

And that is not just enough—that is more than enough. That we have God forever . . . that is more than enough.

# Everyday Surrenders

Surrender does feel costly when our lives are falling apart, but surrender sometimes feels even more difficult in the mundane everyday. And God calls us to trust Him with both. Surrendering to God means we will willingly receive whatever He has for us. It could involve big things like cancer or losing our job, but usually surrender comes in the form of being content with tight budgets, or helping our roommate decide what to wear before she gets picked up for a date when we are single, or staying up with a child all night with a fever.

We mistakenly believe God is holding out on us if He doesn't give us the things on earth we most desire. But God spoke us into being, He poured out the blood of His Son, and He filled us with His Spirit. The depths of God fill the depths of us. He is withholding nothing. He gave us all of Himself. The God of universes gave every piece of Himself for us.

When we begin to see that a God like that is One we want to surrender to, when we see there is nothing more beautiful than someone whose life is God's for the taking, He takes our surrendered lives and pours them out on people who need His grace. But we must first offer Him everything and be content with however He writes our story.

Is God holding out on you?

Who are you, Lord?  &  What do you want for me?

Read Psalm 22. In light of what you read, answer the questions above.

In the next few projects, take time to reflect on the state of your heart and what you have learned about God in this study of David. Think about your hopes for your future as you pursue God's heart in this life and the next.

# engage.

We all have expectations . . . expectations about our life, our marriage, our job, our God. And God in His mercy does let us experience joy in these things, but He gives us something so much more substantial than this short life.

Where have you unknowingly let expectations rob you of joy? Make a list below of unmet expectations in your life. Write what God says your expectations should be for this life.

| | Expectations | What God Says |
|---|---|---|
| Relationships | | |
| Job Opportunities | | |
| God | | |
| Finances | | |
| Other | | |

# dream.

Dream about heaven.

What will you see?

Who will be there?

What will you be doing?

Where will you live?

What do you imagine God will be like?

---

*Then I saw a new heaven and a new earth, for the first heaven and the first earth had passed away, and the sea was no more. And I saw the holy city, new Jerusalem, coming down out of heaven from God, prepared as a bride adorned for her husband. And I heard a loud voice from the throne saying, "Behold, the dwelling place of God is with man. He will dwell with them, and they will be his people, and God himself will be with them as their God. He will wipe away every tear from their eyes, and death shall be no more, neither shall there be mourning, nor crying, nor pain anymore, for the former things have passed away."*

## revelation 21:1–4

# act.

Did not I weep for him whose day was hard?
Was not my soul grieved for the needy?

job 30:25

Ecclesiastes 3:4 says there is a "time to weep, and a time to laugh; a time to mourn, and a time to dance." There is a time for grief and many people you know are in a season of grief. Think of a friend who is suffering.

Write your friend a letter and include passages of Psalms. Take time to hurt with this friend. Christ hurts with us and gives us space to hurt. Be the hands and feet of Christ to someone this week.

# consider.

*Not only that, but we rejoice in our sufferings, knowing that suffering produces endurance, and endurance produces character, and character produces hope.*

**romans 5:3‒4**

Describe a time you have suffered.

Where was God in that season?

How are you different because of that suffering?

What was your hope through that time?

# Conclusion

My sister Brooke named her baby girl Lucy Hope because she knew she would see her again. And in the weeks and months that followed Lucy's death, Brooke clung to God through this verse:

> "The Lᴏʀᴅ is my portion," says my soul,
>> "therefore I will hope in him."

lamentations 3:24

The Lord is enough of a portion to fill our souls. We don't always feel full or remember He is enough. David often questioned God's presence as he suffered. But as we read how David cried out to God, we can sense his soul filling with something real and satisfying. Before long David was praising God because God was his portion. God was enough.

So my sister keeps praying to the God who let her suffer . . . she keeps handing her life over to Him and saying, "Your will be done with us." That is a beautiful thing to say to God: "You have me. Whatever you want to do with my life, I am yours."

> God is our refuge and strength,
>> a very present help in trouble.
> Therefore we will not fear though the earth gives way,
>> though the mountains be moved into the heart of the sea,
> though its waters roar and foam,
>> though the mountains tremble at its swelling.

psalm 46:1–3

# see ::

Watch video lesson 7: SURRENDER

Use streaming instructions
on inside cover or DVD.

Take notes if you like.

# ask ::

Use lesson 7: SURRENDER
Conversation Cards for
group discussion.

notes

# chased down :: 8

*God chased us down through Jesus.*

Work through pages 162–174 on your own before your next group
meeting and before you watch the next video teaching.

What do we long for more than any other thing? The holes every person tries to fill from birth till death are the needs to be known and to be loved. We chase everything trying to fill these God-given holes. He left space in us for Him. That's just plain cool. He made us incomplete without Him and yet we want everything but Him . . . so He came after us.

We had a bed that once was empty, a bottom bunk we never thought would be permanently filled. But we could not shake God's leading to fill that empty bed with a child who needed a home. After embarking on the journey toward our fourth child, one and one-half years would pass before he would fill that bottom bunk. For more than five hundred nights I would kiss my oldest son in the top bunk, look at the neatly made bottom bunk, and hurt and pray for our son who was waking up an ocean away in a little cement room with twenty-five other African toddlers.

I wanted that boy so deeply I would have swum to him.

A four-year-old with no living relatives and not one possession to his name had no idea that across the world, a mom and dad were crying and praying and spending every drop of savings to get to him. He didn't know.

# God's Reach

Most of my life I've either been working hard to please God or feeling guilty for not pleasing Him. But David wasn't possessed by that struggle. Something about David's understanding of our God was different. He experienced something most of us long for more than any other thing: he experienced God's love for him. There was no measuring up, just a God who loved him and saved him.

> I waited patiently for the LORD;
>     he turned to me and heard my cry.
> He lifted me out of the slimy pit,
>     out of the mud and mire;
> he set my feet on a rock
>     and gave me a firm place to stand.

psalm 40:1–2 NIV

I was in a pit, and my striving to get out only took me deeper into it. God reached in for me. God came after me. Courage and obedience and assurance and repentance come only from a God who reached into a pit to save us. They aren't things to strive after. They are the result of knowing a real God who really saved us and then moved in and settled in our souls.

David's life was remarkable only because he believed in God and the God he actually believed in was remarkable.

**God**

chose

adopted

filled

strengthened

enabled

convicted

restored

forgave

established

David.

God made David great. David just let Him.

And through David, God was chasing after all of us. He knit together generations to get to us. He came as an infant to get to us. He died a brutal death to get us.

# study ::

## read ephesians 1:3–14

What did Christ do for us?

What happened to us?

What does that mean for our lives now?

Why would God do this?

---

*But because of his great love for us, God, who is rich in mercy, made us alive with Christ even when we were dead in transgressions—it is by grace you have been saved.*

ephesians 2:4–5 NIV

---

Do you feel unconditionally loved by God?

## Entirely New

Because of Christ, not one thing is the same. We aren't striving to be new. We are just . . . new. The old "us" died with Christ and we came back something entirely different. David lived as if it were all true. Those of us in Christ have not one bit less of God in us than David did, and God is not one bit less powerful now than He was when David was alive. We just don't live as if it were all true.

**God**

chose

adopted

filled

strengthened

enabled

convicted

restored

forgave

established

*us*.

And now we can go live out God in us, brave and obedient and repentant and humble and forgiven, because we are God's. He chased after us, not because we were worthy but because God is just that good.

Who are you, Lord?  What do you want for me?

Read Psalm 40. In light of what you read, answer the questions above.

# reflect.

Go back to the three things you were chasing on page 24 of the Getting Started lesson.

Write them again here.

If you met God today, would you be proud these were the pursuits of your life?

May we have one pursuit. One.

Jesus.

# worship.

Download a Hillsong United song, Chris Tomlin's "Amazing Grace," or U2's "40."
Listen to it in your car or while you're walking and just thank Jesus. Sing and pray and
worship a God who loves us no matter our mistakes and pursues us while we run after
everything but Him.

# commit.

The consequences of God's love are great. He, in most ways, has wrecked the life I was planning to have. But He promises a better life. He promises to build stories that last forever through us and He promises to live life with us, in us and through us.

What are you
leaving behind?

What are you
moving toward?

# respond.

Spend an hour with a good friend or your spouse this week and share with him or her what God is teaching you.

What has most convicted you while studying the life of David?

What did you discover you believed about God that was incorrect?

What have you learned about His character?

How do you want to live in light of this?

# Wrapping Up

That bottom bunk bed I told you about isn't empty anymore. Last night after stories and prayers and giggles, with new, broken English my African son comforted himself with this truth:

"Mom, when I was sad at the orphanage, you were working hard to get me."

I pulled him so tight and he let me. "Oh, we wanted you Cooper. So much that it hurt inside. We had to get you. While you were waiting we were chasing you down."

God has chased us down and none of our pursuits, however vain, could make Him love us less. David loved God and God loved David. Courage, obedience, belief, repentance, and surrender all flowed out of the depth of their love for each other, from the depth of their relationship. This is why we can't muster these qualities up on our own. They come from a source. The source is a relationship with God. And if we weren't so numb to those words, we would come out of our skin with excitement that this is even possible. A relationship with the God who speaks planets and souls and stars into place . . . that is unthinkable.

When I meet God, I want to face Him completely out of breath from having chased Him with these few days I have on earth. On that day, I want to have lived what I say I believe. I want to have talked to God more than I talk to anyone else. I want to have trusted God and followed Him anywhere.

May we run after God today with the same faith we will have the day our faith becomes sight. I have a feeling every other pursuit will feel futile on that day.

Let's live like God is real and heaven is coming.

*For now we see in a mirror dimly, but then face to face. Now I know in part; then I shall know fully, even as I have been fully known.*

## 1 corinthians 13:12

# see ::

Watch video lesson 8:
CHASED DOWN

Use streaming instructions
on inside cover or DVD.

Take notes if you like.

# ask

Use lesson 8: CHASED DOWN
Conversation Cards for
group discussion.

# how to find god

Humanity had a perfect relationship with God until sin entered the world through Adam and Eve. With sin came the certainty of death and eternal separation from God. The penalty had to be paid. But at the same moment that He named the punishment for the first sin, God issued His promise to provide a way for us to return to Him.

Our sin was to be placed on the perfect sacrifice. God would send His own blameless, perfect Son to bear our sin and suffer our deserved fate—to get us back.

Jesus came, fulfilling thousands of years of prophecy, lived a perfect life, and died a gruesome death, satisfying the payment for our sin. Then after three days, He defeated death, rose from the grave, and is now seated with the Father.

Anyone who accepts the blood of Jesus for the forgiveness of their sin can be adopted as a child of God. To each one who believes, God issues His very own Spirit to seal and empower us to live this life for and with Him.

We were made for God, and He gave everything so that our souls could finally and forever find their rest in Him.

If you have never trusted Christ for the forgiveness of your sins, you can do that this moment. Just tell Him you need Him and tell Him you choose to trust Him as your Lord and Savior.

*She will chase after her lovers but not catch them; she will look for them but not find them.*

**hosea** 2:7 NIV

# leader's guide

## Leaders,

I am excited to partner with you in your efforts to pour into the lives of women! I pray that these few short pages will help to equip and prepare you to lead this study. Many of you may have led plenty of groups in the past, or perhaps this is the first you've led. Whichever the case, this is a spiritual calling and you are entering spiritual places with these women—and spiritual callings and places need spiritual power.

My husband, Zac, always says, "Changed lives, change lives." If you are not first aware of your own need for life change, the women around you won't see their need. If you allow God into the inner struggles of your heart, the women following you will be much more likely to let Him into theirs. These women do not need to see bright and shiny, perfectly poised people; they need to see people who are a mess and daily dependent on God for their hope and strength.

David was a wild, passionate warrior king, whose own messy story I had heard and whose psalms I had read a thousand times, but when I began to look a bit more closely at the life of this man, something about the way he related to God just wrecked me. His view of God was so big. David actually believed God was real and he lived like it. He chased after God's heart (Acts 13:22). And I think as a generation of women, we are longing to do the same. We want to believe God is real and to live like it. We are tired of chasing everything else under the sun. We are tired of chasing wind (Ecclesiastes 1:14). We want to chase Him.

This is not a study for people who want to play it safe. This study will mess with you, just as it messed with me, because we all are chasing things other than God, and when you look into the life of someone chasing God Himself, God alone, you start craving Him too. I want a life like David's, brave and dependent and full of worship. He had a relationship with God unlike any other in Scripture and, honestly, unlike any other I've ever seen. I want to know God like he did. I want to trust God like he did.

I think many of us are tired and though we would like to please God, it feels like it would take a lot of effort to do that. *Chase* is an experiment in what it is God truly wants from us. The more I understand what God has done, the more I quit striving and simply rest in Him. David chased God, but part of them meant resting in the work of God, in God's favor, in the plans God had written for him. Whether you are running from God or working your tail off to please Him, David's journey will challenge your view of God.

Let's chase.

*Jennie*

# the vision

1. That we would see to uncover the things we are chasing on this earth instead of God Himself.

---

*I have seen everything that is done under the sun, and behold, all is vanity and a striving after wind.*

## Ecclesiastes 1:14

---

2. That we would see that God wants us to love and chase Him above every other thing on earth and that our souls were built to be full of God. This is why nothing else satisfies. We were made for God.

> Know that the LORD, he is God!
>> It is he who made us, and we are his;
>> we are his people, and the sheep of his pasture.
>
> Psalm 100:3

We were made for God and He has called us to love Him above every single other thing.

*You shall have no other gods before me.*

## Exodus 20:3

*You shall love the Lord your God with all your heart and with all your soul and with all your strength and with all your mind.*

## Luke 10:27

3. That women would be pointed to God, a God worth dying for. The rest of this leader's guide is aimed at equipping you to point the women of your group to God in ways that will change their lives.

# preparing yourself to lead a group

1. **Pray:** Pray like the world is ending, pray like this is the last chance for people to know Him, pray like your lives and futures depend on it, pray like the future of souls in heaven is at stake . . . pray like you need God.

Pray for your women:

:: That God would show them the things they are chasing instead of God Himself.

:: That they would feel safe to open up and process.

:: That they would want more of God and that God would meet them.

:: That the conversation would be focused on God.

:: That we would be humble displays of God's grace to these women.

:: That God would come and fall on your time together.

:: That many would come to a saving faith as they see God for who He is.

2. **Lean on God.** Allow the Holy Spirit to lead every moment together. We have provided you with tools that we will discuss in the next section; however, they are only tools to use as the Spirit leads you and your time together. God will have unique agendas for each of your groups as you depend on Him. Lean into your own weakness and into His strength and direction.

   When Jesus left His disciples to go back to His Father in heaven, He essentially said, *Don't go anywhere until you have the helper I will send you* (see Acts 1:4–5). That helper was the Holy Spirit. We need to obey that same command. We shouldn't begin until we are doing so with the power of the Holy Spirit within us. He is real and available and waiting to flood our lives and the lives of those around us as we serve and speak. But we have to wait for Him to speak, ask Him if we should speak and what we should speak, and ask Him what to do in different situations. God wants us to need Him and to depend on His Spirit. If this is not how you live on a daily basis, begin today.

3. **Be transparent.** If you choose not to be vulnerable, no one else will be. If you desire women to feel safe with you and your group, be vulnerable. This is not an optional assignment. This is your calling as you lead these women.

4. **Listen but also lead.** Listen as women share struggles. Some women are taking a tremendous risk in being vulnerable with you. Protect them by not interrupting and by instead empathizing. Do not feel the need to speak after each person shares. After most women have shared their answers to a question, turn it back to the scripture from the study guide and help them process the truth and hope in their struggles. Avoid lecturing, but do bring the women back to truth.

5. **Model trust.** Show your group how you are applying these difficult lessons. Ask God to convict you and lead out with how you are processing change in your own life.

# the study

## Session Tools, How to Use Them, and Format

This study is uniquely designed to work in any venue or location. I envision women leading this in their homes, on campuses, even in their workplaces. Church buildings are the traditional format for group Bible studies and *Chase* will be effective within the church walls, but the bigger dream is that women would find this study useful in reaching their friends, neighbors, and coworkers.

Whether you find yourself with 150 women in a church auditorium or with a few neighbors in your living room, this study is designed for small groups of women to process truth within their souls. Because of the depth of the questions and topics, it is essential your group be small enough to share. A maximum of eight women in each group is ideal, fewer is preferable. If you are in a larger group, divide into smaller groups with volunteer facilitators. With the help of the leader's guide and the Ask conversation cards, those smaller groups should still prove successful with a little support.

## Tools Needed

**Study Guide.** Each study guide comes with leader's guide and streaming video access. Every participant will need a Bible study guide. Distribute the books at your first group meeting, or have participants purchase and bring their guides on their own.

**Conversation Card Deck.** Group discussion questions and memory verse card for each session.

# How To Use Your Tools

Each lesson is divided into three main sections:

## Study

Point out the weekly Study section, followed by the Projects. These can be completed in one sitting or spaced throughout the week. The Study lessons in the book (except for the Introduction lesson) should be completed between group meetings.

The lessons are interactive, designed to help people study Scripture for themselves and apply it to their lives. The Projects in the Bible study guide provide creative options for applying Scripture. Some of these experiences may push participants outside their comfort zones. Encourage them to be brave and tackle the challenge. Make sure to discuss the Projects at each group meeting.

## See

Watch the short, engaging video teaching to introduce the lesson via streaming or DVD to set the tone for your time together, and challenge your group to apply Scripture. If your group members want to take notes, encourage them to use the Notes page opposite each SEE title page. Each study guide includes instructions for personal access to streaming video on the inside front cover. This is perfect for anyone who might miss a group gathering, want to rewatch any of the video teaching, or if your group needs to meet on shortened time.

# Ask

After the video teaching is complete, ask the group if anything in particular stood out while you prepare the Conversation Cards.

The Conversation Cards provide a unique way to jump-start honest discussion. Each week's cards are labeled with the appropriate lesson title and can be used after the video or teaching time. The following is a suggested step-by-step way to use the cards.

:: Begin by laying out the Scripture Cards for that specific week.
:: Direct each group member to take a card.
:: Go over the Ground Rules each week. (Ground rules are found on page 11 and on the back of the Instruction card.)
:: Take turns presenting the question on each card to the group.

Provide adequate time for everyone in your group to respond to each question.

Don't feel pressured to read and answer every card. Be sensitive to the leading of the Holy Spirit and your time constraints. Remind the group that what they share and how they share are entirely personal decisions. No one should be forced to answer every card.

NOTE: Make use of this leader's guide to facilitate a great Bible study experience for your group. It will help you point people to the overarching theme for each lesson and will give you specific suggestions on how to share the truth and foster discussion.

## Session Format

This eight-week study is designed to go deep very quickly. Since women are busy and have full lives, the beauty of this study is it can be led in a living room over a one-hour lunch, or in a church Bible study spread out over two and a half hours. If you have the flexibility, extend the time of sharing in small groups. A frequent complaint is, "We wish we had more time to share." When the group is given deep questions and space to reflect and respond, you'll be surprised how beautiful and plentiful the conversations will be.

You will be the best judge of what time and format works for your group. However, here is a suggested schedule for each group meeting.

## OPEN—Personal study discussion [20-35 minutes]:

After welcoming everyone and opening in prayer, you may choose to begin by having the women discuss their personal reflections as they have worked through the study guide and Scripture that week. If you have more than eight members, break into small groups for this discussion time before reconvening for the video/teaching time.

## SEE—Video teaching [video: 8-12 minutes]:

Watch the DVD to provide a foundation for that week's lesson and to help transition to transparent sharing using the Ask conversation cards. Each video is approximately 8–12 minutes long. If you are supplying teaching in addition to the videos, we recommend you begin with your teaching and then play the video.

NOTE TO CHURCH GROUPS: Due to the nature of this study, we strongly suggest that each group have no more than 8–12 women and that you have a kit for each group.

## ASK—Conversation Cards [30-75 minutes]:

Especially if there are more than eight group members, divide into smaller groups and have women go through the Ask conversation cards. This will be a time of deep sharing and discussion that is important to understanding how to apply all that has been learned that week. If your small group needs an extra deck of Ask cards, they are available for purchase at www.thomasnelson.com.

## CLOSE—Closing (5-10 minutes)

Pray as a group and encourage everyone to engage in the Study before meeting again.

# leading your group: tips and things to watch out for

## Guiding Conversation

You may come across some challenges when leading a group conversation. Normally these challenges fall into two categories. In both situations people will need encouragement and grace from you as a leader. As with everything in this study, seek the Holy Spirit's guidance as you interact with your group members.

1. **Dominating the conversation:** If one woman seems to be dominating the conversation or going into detail that makes the rest of the group uncomfortable, gently interrupt her if necessary and thank her for sharing. Avoid embarrassing her in front of the group. Ask if there is anyone else who would like to share in response to the original question asked (not to necessarily respond to the woman who was just speaking). If the problem persists, talk with the woman outside of the group time. Affirm her for her vulnerability and willingness to share and be prepared to refer her for more help if the need arises.

2. **Not sharing as much as the others:** If you notice there is a woman who seems to not be as talkative as the others in the group, you may try gently asking for her input directly at some point in the conversation. Some women are naturally shyer than others; don't try to force them into an extroverted role, but do let them know their input is valuable to the group. Remind them of the goals of the study and how being vulnerable with one another is one of the ways God shapes us spiritually. If a woman is just not interested in being in the study and is holding the rest of the group back, meet with her outside the group setting to discuss her further involvement.

Keep in mind that no two women are alike, but keep the best interests of the group in mind as you lead. Encourage group members to follow the Ground Rules for Group Discussion Time (below and also found on page 11 in the study guide.) Review these items together as often as needed in order to keep the conversation on track:

:: *Be concise.* Share your answers to the questions while protecting others' time for sharing. Be thoughtful. Don't be afraid to share with the group, but try not to dominate the conversation.

:: *Keep group members' stories confidential.* Many things your group members share are things they are choosing to share with you, not with your husband or other friends. Protect each other by not allowing anything shared in the group to leave the group.

:: *Rely on Scripture for truth.* We are prone to use conventional, worldly wisdom as truth. While there is value in that, this is not the place. If you feel led to respond, please only respond with God's truth and Word, not "advice."

:: *No counseling.* Protect the group by not directing all attention on solving one person's problem. This is the place for confessing and discovery and applying truth together as a group. Your group leader will be able to direct you to more help outside the group time if you need it. Don't be afraid to ask for help.

## When to Refer

Some of the women in your care may be suffering beyond the point you feel able to help. This study may bring the pain of circumstances or behaviors to the surface. To leave women in this state would be more damaging than helpful. Don't try to take on problems you do not feel equipped to handle. If you sense that a woman may need more help, follow up and refer her to someone.

:: Check with your church or pastor for names of trusted Christian counselors. Some major indicators of this need would be: depression, anxiety, suicide, abuse, broken marriage. These are the obvious ones, but honestly, some women who are stuck in hurt from their past, minor depression, or fear could also benefit from counseling. I believe counseling is beneficial for many. So keep a stash of names for anyone you may feel needs to process further with a professional.

:: Look for the nearest Celebrate Recovery group and offer to attend the first meeting with her (www.celebraterecovery.com).

:: Suggest further resources and help to make a plan for their future growth and well-being.

:: Communicate with the leadership at your church about how to proceed with care.

:: Do not abandon these hurting women in a vulnerable place. This may be the first time they have opened up about painful hurts or patterns. Own their care and see it through. If they have landed in your group, God has assigned them to you for this season, until they are trusted to the care of someone else. Even then, continue to check in on them.

# types of learners

Hopefully, you will be blessed to be leading this study with a group diverse in age, experience, and style. While the benefits of coming together as a diverse group to discuss God outweigh the challenges by a mile, there are often distinctions in learning styles. Just be aware and consider some of the differences in two types of learning styles that may be represented. (These are obviously generalizations, and each woman as an individual will express her own unique communication style, but in general these are common characteristics.)

## Experiential Learners

There are women who are more transparent, don't like anything cheesy, want to go deep quickly, and are passionate. Make a safe environment for them by being transparent yourself and engaging their hearts. These women may not care as much about head knowledge and may care more deeply how knowledge about God applies to their lives. They want to avoid being put in a box. Keep the focus on applying truth to their lives and they will stay engaged. Don't preach to them; be real and show them through your experiences how to truly chase after God.

## Pragmatic Learners

These women are more accustomed to a traditional, inductive, or precept approach to Bible study. They have a high value for truth and authority but may not place as high a value on the emotional aspects of confessing sin and being vulnerable. To them it may feel unnecessary or dramatic. Keep the focus on the truth of Scripture. These women keep truth in the forefront of their lives and play a valuable role in discipleship.

***

Because this study is different from traditional studies, some women may need more time to get used to the approach. The goal is still to make God big in our lives, to know and love Him more and to deal with sin by instructing with Scripture. These are the goals for all believers; we all just approach it in unique ways to reach unique types of people. I actually wrote this study praying it could reach both types of learners. I am one who lives with a foot in both worlds, trying to apply the deep truths I gained in seminary in an experiential way. I pray that this study would deeply engage the heart and the mind, and that we would be people who worship God in spirit and in truth, not just learning about sin but going to war with it together.

Common struggles like fear, stress, anger, shame, and insecurity are not respecters of age, religion, or income level. These struggles are human and I have seen *Chase* transcend the typical boundaries of Christian and seeker, young and old, single and married, needy and comfortable, bringing these women together and to God in a unique and powerful way.

In the following pages and notes for each *Chase* lesson, I hope I have given you enough guidance that you do not feel lost, but enough freedom to depend on the Holy Spirit. These are only suggestions, but hopefully these notes will help surface themes and goals to guide you through your discussion of group members' homework and through the discussion of the Ask conversation cards. The video, homework, and cards should provide more than enough material for great discussions, but stay on track and be sure people are walking away with hope and truth.

# getting started : chase :: 1

*After chasing everything this world has to offer,*
*nothing is more satisfying than God.*

During this first meeting you will be getting to know each other, handing out the study guides, walking through the Instructions and Expectations (found on page 10 of the study guide), walking through the Getting Started lesson (found on page 19 of the study guide), and watching the first video.

Here are some general goals and thoughts for your time together this week:

:: Make the women feel safe.

:: Get to know each other and the things you each are chasing.

:: Set expectations for the study.

:: Instruct group members on how you will be using the study guide, watching the video teaching, and engaging in group discussion with the Ask conversation cards.

:: Create a need for this study in their lives by helping them see that we all are chasing something.

:: Stress that God is longing for a real relationship with each of us.

:: Introduce David from pages 13–17.

**LEADER:** This first session's suggested format is different from the others since it is your first meeting and there is no homework to review.

# OPEN

Welcome the participants to your group and take a few moments for introductions. Briefly share about yourself and allow others to do the same. After introductions, lead the group in prayer.

1. Together take some time to read the Introduction, Instructions and Expectations, and explain and show the group their individual access to streaming video so everyone can keep up with the study, regardless of an unavoidable missed gathering.

2. Turn to the Getting Started lesson in the study guide and either read aloud or to yourselves and discuss.

2. When you reach page 24 in the Getting Started lesson of the study guide, have participants choose the three things their hearts are chasing most. Give everyone time to think about this and write down in their guide their three things.

3. If you are in a large group, break into small groups and give each person the chance to open up about the three things they are chasing right now. Leaders, share first and be transparent.

4. Gather the group again for the video teaching.

# SEE (video teaching)

View video session one: GETTING STARTED: CHASE

# ASK (Discussion Time)

Transition to the Conversation Cards for discussion. Remember to begin with the Scripture card and end by stressing the scriptural truth group members can apply to their lives as a result of what they discuss in your group time.

The cards for this week are labeled "CHASE" on the front. Lead participants to choose, answer, and discuss the questions on the cards. (You can review the instructions for using the cards in ASK on page 192.)

---

*I have seen everything that is done under the sun, and behold, all is vanity and a striving after wind.*

## Ecclesiastes 1:14

---

# CLOSE

Close by asking the group to write down three things:

:: one thing they learned from this session;
:: one reason they are excited about this study;
:: one question they have moving forward.

Briefly discuss their responses. Do so with little or no commentary but paying close attention to the answers. If time allows, close by praying specifically for each person in your group, using one of each person's responses as the focus of your prayer for them.

# identity :: 2

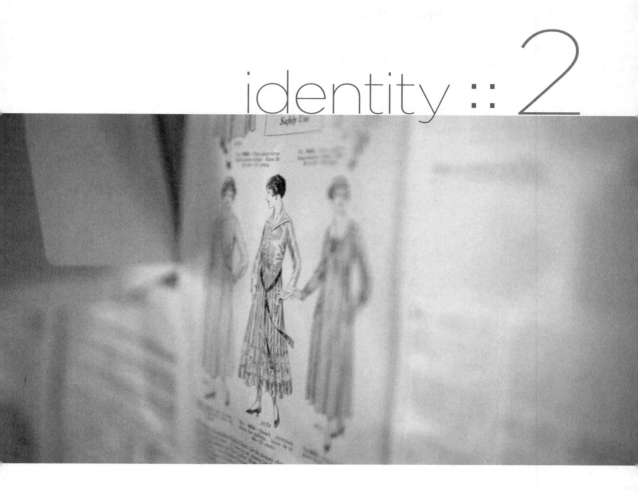

*What if the identity we are all chasing has already been given to us by God.*

**MAIN IDEA:** The identity we are chasing will fail us again and again, but the identity that God gives, if we will grasp it, is substantial and changes everything.

This week we will look at one reason why we are chasing the things of this world: we are looking for a strong identity. We want to know we matter and that we are unique. David lived with a very strong sense of identity and it began by believing fully in what God said about him.

Here are some general goals and thoughts for your time together this week:

:: Identify and define some of the things we try to put our identity in.

:: Discover how David's calling was similar to God's calling for us.

:: Discuss the things God says about His commitment to us.

:: A secure identity comes from a high view of God, not from an inflated self-esteem.

**MAIN GOAL:** Lead people to a right view of their own depravity and failed identity apart from a God who restores them and gives them a secure, monumental identity.

# OPEN—Personal study discussion

Here are some suggested places to focus as you go over the homework together. Ask the group:

:: Share what you learned as you studied David in 1 Samuel 16.

:: How did Psalm 23 speak to you based on where you are in your life right now?

:: Discuss your response to Project 2.

:: What else did you learn as you studied and interacted with the lesson and Scripture this week?

# SEE (video teaching)

View video session two: IDENTITY

# ASK (Discussion Time)

Transition to the Conversation Cards for discussion. Remember to begin with the Scripture card and end by stressing the scriptural truth group members can apply to their lives as a result of what they discuss in your group time.

The cards for this week are labeled "IDENTITY" on the front. Lead participants to choose, answer, and discuss the questions on the cards. (You can review the instructions for using the cards in ASK on page 192.)

---

*In love he predestined us for adoption as sons through Jesus Christ, according to the purpose of his will, to the praise of his glorious grace, with which he has blessed us in the Beloved.*

## Ephesians 1:4–6

---

# CLOSE

Read this week's Scripture memory verse aloud to the group and instruct the group to commit each verse to memory each week as best they can. Pray together and dismiss.

# courage :: 3

*Courage is the strength that leads us to act in spite of opposition.*

**MAIN IDEA:** Truly courageous people have nothing to lose. They fear God and therefore they fear nothing else.

This week we studied the account of David and Goliath, and hopefully everyone gained new insight into this familiar story. When we draw from God's strength, we can act in spite of opposition.

Here are some general goals and thoughts for your time together this week:

:: Create a restlessness in the women, so that they don't settle for mediocre lives.

:: Our motive for action must be the glory of God; create a burden in your group members for the glory of God on this earth.

:: What does it look like to live with a single-minded desire to see God and please Him?

:: Courage is not the absence of fear; it is believing God despite fear.

**MAIN GOAL:** Push people to a view of a God so sovereign that they in turn trust Him even with the things they most fear losing.

# OPEN—Personal study discussion

Here are some suggested places to focus as you go over the homework together. Ask the group:

:: Discuss 1 Samuel 17. Describe the difference between the Israelite army and David.

:: What are everyday fears for you?

:: What was God speaking to you through Psalm 27?

:: Share your drawings from Project 3.

:: What else did you learn as you studied and interacted with the lesson and Scripture this week?

# SEE (video teaching)

View video session three: COURAGE

# ASK (Discussion Time)

Transition to the Conversation Cards for discussion. Remember to begin with the Scripture card and end by stressing the scriptural truth group members can apply to their lives as a result of what they discuss in your group time.

The cards for this week are labeled "COURAGE" on the front. Lead participants to choose, answer, and discuss the questions on the cards. (You can review the instructions for using the cards in ASK on page 192.)

---

*If God is for us, who can be against us? He who did not spare his own Son, but gave him up for us all, how will he not also with him graciously give us all things? . . . As it is written, "For your sake we are being killed all the day long; we are regarded as sheep to be slaughtered." No, in all these things we are more than conquerors through him who loved us. For I am sure that neither death nor life, nor angels nor rulers, nor things present nor things to come, nor powers, nor height nor depth, nor anything else in all creation, will be able to separate us from the love of God in Christ Jesus our Lord.*

## Romans 8:31–32, 36–38

---

# CLOSE

Read this week's Scripture memory verse aloud to the group and instruct the group to commit each verse to memory each week as best they can. Pray together and dismiss.

# obedience :: 4

*The more we trust God, the more we obey Him.*

**MAIN IDEA:** A trusting relationship with God will cause us to desire to obey.

This week we studied a potentially controversial subject: obedience. We asked God to reveal to us whether we are approaching obedience in the way He desires—out of a heart of love for Him rather than out of a desire to look good to other people.

Here are some general goals and thoughts for your time together this week:

:: Help women see that our view of God will determine our trust in Him and our trust in Him will determine our desire to obey Him.

:: If we know God and trust Him, we will obey no matter the cost, even if it feels foolish.

:: Scripture is the first place we understand God's desires for us, and recognizing God's voice through His Spirit's leading is the second.

:: Obedience is not motivated by fear or performance but by a loving and trusting relationship with God.

**MAIN GOAL:** Lead people to a right understanding of Christ's work on our behalf, the freedom His work brings, and the desire it brings to obey and trust God.

# OPEN—Personal study discussion

Here are some suggested places to focus as you go over the homework together. Ask the group:

:: What were the differences between Saul and David in the passages we studied (1 Samuel 15:1–31 and 1 Samuel 23:2–14)?

:: What did you feel as you read Psalm 63 this week?

:: Which project stood out to you most this week?

:: What else did you learn as you studied and interacted with the lesson and Scripture this week?

# SEE (video teaching)

View video session four: OBEDIENCE

## ASK (Discussion Time)

Transition to the Conversation Cards for discussion. Remember to begin with the Scripture card and end by stressing the scriptural truth group members can apply to their lives as a result of what they discuss in your group time.

The cards for this week are labeled "OBEDIENCE" on the front. Lead participants to choose, answer, and discuss the questions on the cards. (You can review the instructions for using the cards in ASK on page 192.)

*My sheep hear My voice, and I know them, and they follow Me.*

## John 10:27

## CLOSE

Read this week's Scripture memory verse aloud to the group and instruct the group to commit each verse to memory each week as best they can. Pray together and dismiss.

belief :: 5

*How we live every second of every day will flow out of what we believe about God.*

**MAIN IDEA:** Faith is the basis of a relationship with God and it is the basis of our salvation, and most of us are afraid to ever express doubt. Yet all of us doubt at some point.

This week we were probably a little uncomfortable as we faced the reality of our doubts. We learned that doubts are likely inevitable, but that the reality of God far outweighs those doubts when we ask Him to help our unbelief.

Here are some general goals and thoughts for your time together this week:

:: Explain that the Davidic Covenant promised an eternal kingdom through David that would result in the ultimate King, Jesus Christ.

:: Do we really believe all that we say we believe? Because if we did, it would change our entire lives.

:: Our doubts are keeping us from God.

:: The result of believing all that God says about us will be gratitude and worship.

:: Nothing matters more than what we believe about God.

:: We can ask God for more faith. We can go to Him with our doubts.

**MAIN GOAL:** Lead people to admit their doubts, to wrestle through them, and to turn to God with their questions.

## OPEN—Personal study discussion

Here are some suggested places to focus as you go over the homework together. Ask the group:

:: Talk about the covenant God made with David in 2 Samuel 7, and discuss David's reaction to such a big, supernatural promise.

:: Discuss how that promise affects us today through Christ.

:: What are some of the doubts you expressed in Project 1?

:: What else did you learn as you studied and interacted with the lesson and Scripture this week?

## SEE (video teaching)

View video session five: BELIEF

# ASK (Discussion Time)

Transition to the Conversation Cards for discussion. Remember to begin with the Scripture card and end by stressing the scriptural truth group members can apply to their lives as a result of what they discuss in your group time.

The cards for this week are labeled "BELIEF" on the front. Lead participants to choose, answer, and discuss the questions on the cards. (You can review the instructions for using the cards in ASK on page 192.)

---

*Have you believed because you have seen me? Blessed are those who have not seen and yet have believed.*

## John 20:29

---

# CLOSE

Read this week's Scripture memory verse aloud to the group and instruct the group to commit each verse to memory each week as best they can. Pray together and dismiss.

# repentance :: 6

*It is God's mercy to show us our sin and lead us to repentance.*

**MAIN IDEA:** Seeing our sin is the first thing we must do to see our need for God.

This week we studied the account of David and Bathsheba, and confronted our own responses to sin—do we hide from our sin in shame or do we deny our sin with pride? We learned that the only way to truly deal with sin is to take it to God with a heart of repentance. He will never run out of grace for the repentant heart.

Here are some general goals and thoughts for your time together this week:

:: We do not comprehend how much we have offended God, every one of us.

:: There will never be absence of sin, and all sin is the same to God, so we are all in need of repentance.

:: God draws near to the brokenhearted and near to the contrite heart.

:: Belief in the life and death of Christ is our hope. Jesus eliminates shame and pride.

**MAIN GOAL:** Lead people to confession and repentance and forgiveness. Push them to abandon pretending.

## OPEN—Personal study discussion

Here are some suggested places to focus as you go over the homework together. Ask the group:

::  What did you think of David's mistakes in 2 Samuel 11 and 12? What stood out about his repentance?

::  Read portions of Psalm 32 and contrast confessed sin with unconfessed sin.

::  Share your drawings from Project 3.

::  "Against you, you only, have I sinned" (Psalm 51:4). Do you find yourself in this prayer?

::  What else did you learn as you studied and interacted with the lesson and Scripture this week?

## SEE (video teaching)

View video session six: REPENTANCE

## ASK (Discussion Time)

Transition to the Conversation Cards for discussion. Remember to begin with the Scripture card and end by stressing the scriptural truth group members can apply to their lives as a result of what they discuss in your group time.

The cards for this week are labeled "REPENTANCE" on the front. Lead participants to choose, answer, and discuss the questions on the cards. (You can review the instructions for using the cards in ASK on page 192.)

*Those who are well have no need of a physician, but those who are sick. I came not to call the righteous, but sinners.*

Mark 2:17

## CLOSE

Read this week's Scripture memory verse aloud to the group and instruct the group to commit each verse to memory each week as best they can. Pray together and dismiss.

# surrender :: 7

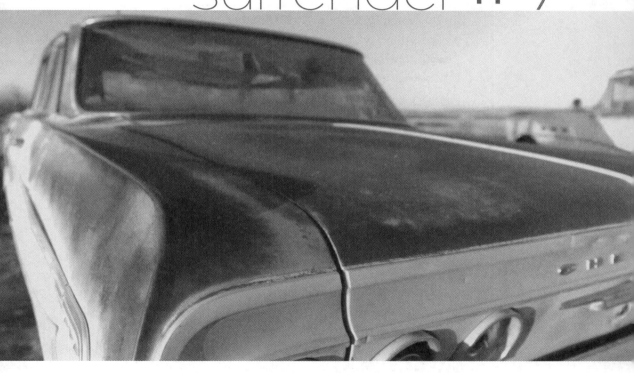

*Surrender to God is not dictated by our circumstances.*

**MAIN IDEA:** Receiving whatever God has for us is part of faith and trust in God. This includes receiving suffering, with an understanding that this life is not all there is.

This week drove home the fact that chasing after God with everything we have doesn't mean we won't suffer. We were faced with this hard truth and had to take a look at ourselves to examine whether we really trust God.

Here are some general goals and thoughts for your time together this week:

:: Help the women understand that we don't get to claim rights. "Whatever the LORD pleases, he does, in heaven and on earth (Psalm 135:6).

:: Our joy is found in our salvation, not in this life.

:: We surrender our lives to God and receive whatever He has for us because He is God.

:: We are afraid to suffer. Suffering is a part of this world and this life, and God wants to use suffering to make us more holy.

**MAIN GOAL:** Lead people to surrender their lives fully to God rather than fighting for control. Help them see their need to follow God's plans for them, whatever those plans are.

# OPEN—Personal study discussion

Here are some suggested places to focus as you go over the homework together. Ask the group:

:: David's suffering was extreme. How do you imagine his view of God grew in such a difficult season of his life?

:: Is God enough for you? If so, what are some ways you know this is true? If it isn't true for you right now, what did you learn this week that challenges you in this area?

:: What are some of the things you learn from David's faith through his suffering? Discuss Psalm 22.

:: Talk through some of the expectations you listed in Project 1.

:: What else did you learn as you studied and interacted with the lesson and Scripture this week?

# SEE (video teaching)

View video session seven: SURRENDER

# ASK (Discussion Time)

Transition to the Conversation Cards for discussion. Remember to begin with the Scripture card and end by stressing the scriptural truth group members can apply to their lives as a result of what they discuss in your group time.

The cards for this week are labeled "SURRENDER" on the front. Lead participants to choose, answer, and discuss the questions on the cards. (You can review the instructions for using the cards in ASK on page 192.)

*And going a little farther, he fell on the ground and prayed that, if it were possible, the hour might pass from him. And he said, "Abba, Father, all things are possible for you. Remove this cup from me. Yet not what I will, but what you will."*

# Mark 14:35–36

# CLOSE

Read this week's Scripture memory verse aloud to the group and instruct the group to commit each verse to memory each week as best they can. Pray together and dismiss.

# chased down :: 8

*God chased us down through Jesus.*

**MAIN IDEA:** While we are running after God, in reality He is the One running after us. Knowing that an infinite God is running after us to save us changes and wrecks every other piece of our lives. What was so remarkable about David? He lived like God was chasing him.

This week as we concluded this study, we realized that all this time God has been chasing us—despite the cost—to make us a part of His family. We are challenged to live like David did and allow God to chase us down.

Here are some general goals and thoughts for your time together this week:

:: Explain that God is the One who made David great. He is the One who makes us great.

:: We don't have to strive to measure up. God loves us and wants us, not our performance.

:: God the Father chased us down through Christ.

:: Allow God to chase you. Feel His love for you.

**MAIN GOAL:** Lead people to a view of God so beautiful and moving that they would do anything for Him.

# OPEN—Personal study discussion

Here are some suggested places to focus as you go over the homework together. Ask the group:

:: Read Ephesians 1:3–14 together and then stop and pray, thanking God for all that He has done for us in this passage.

:: Do you feel unconditionally loved by God? Discuss.

:: Look through Project 1. Share how your perspective has shifted since the first week.

:: What else did you learn as you studied and interacted with the lesson and Scripture this week?

# SEE (video teaching)

View video session eight: CHASED DOWN

## ASK (Discussion Time)

Transition to the Conversation Cards for discussion. Remember to begin with the Scripture card and end by stressing the scriptural truth group members can apply to their lives as a result of what they discuss in your group time.

The cards for this week are labeled "CHASED DOWN" on the front. Lead participants to choose, answer, and discuss the questions on the cards. (You can review the instructions for using the cards in ASK on page 192.)

---

*But because of his great love for us, God, who is rich in mercy, made us alive with Christ even when we were dead in transgressions—it is by grace you have been saved.*

## Ephesians 2:4–5 NIV

---

## CLOSE

Read this week's Scripture memory verse aloud to the group and instruct the group to commit each verse to memory each week as best they can. Pray together and dismiss.

# Also Available from Jennie Allen

### Building Deep Community in a Lonely World

This seven-session video Bible study looks at the original community in Genesis and the Trinity to see how God intended for us to live in community all along.

### The Places We Get Stuck & the God Who Sets Us Free

Stuck is an eight-session video Bible study leading women through the invisible struggles that we fight and to the God who has to set us free.

### Identify the Threads of Your Life

In this eight-session video Bible study using the story of Joseph, Jennie explains how his suffering, gifts, story, and relationships fit into the greater story of God—and how your story can do the same.

### What the Bible Tells Us About Our Emotions

This six-session video Bible study teaches how your emotions actually help you notice what's wrong and connect with God and others more deeply.

### You are Enough Because Jesus is Enough.

In this eight-session video Bible study, Jennie Allen walks through key passages in the Gospel of John that demonstrate how Jesus is enough. We don't have to prove anything because Jesus has proven everything.

### Stopping the Spiral of Toxic Thoughts

In this six-session, video Bible study, Jennie inspires and equips us to transform our emotions, our outlook, and even our circumstances by taking control of our thoughts.

Visit JennieAllen.com for more info. Available wherever books & Bibles are sold.

# We Aren't Supposed to Be This Lonely.

But you don't have to stay there. Let's find your people.

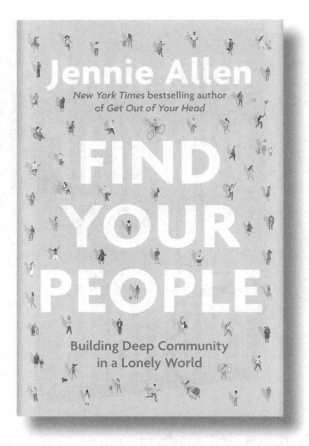

You were created to play, engage, adventure, and explore—with others. In *Find Your People*, you'll discover exactly how to dive into the deep end and experience the full wonder of community. Because while the ache of loneliness is real, it doesn't have to be your reality.

WATERBROOK

waterbrookmultnomah.com

# You are in charge of your thoughts.
## *They are not in charge of you.*

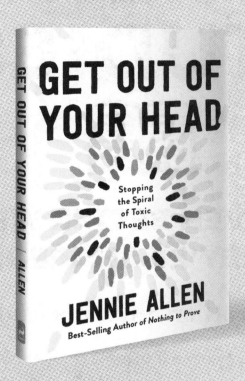

*Get Out of Your Head: Stopping the Spiral of Toxic Thoughts* is a Biblical guide to discovering how to submit our minds to Christ because how we think shapes how we live. As we surrender every thought to Jesus, the promises of God flood our lives in profound ways.

Visit **getoutofyourheadbook.com** for info about *Get Out of Your Head.*

Available wherever books are sold.